Kuberne

C000133957

*Complete Guide to Kubernetes
from Beginner to Advanced*

*(With Simple Practice Projects
To Perfect Your Skills)*

Craig Berg

Introduction

This book shall give you knowledge that'll help you master working with Containers and cloud computing using *Google Kubernetes.*

In the first sections of the book, we will cover what Kubernetes is, its usage, and the pros of using it.

In later sections, you'll learn how to create Kubernetes clusters and how each component works with each other. After learning this, we shall then learn how to run containers in Kubernetes and much more.

NOTE: Although we shall not explicitly cover it, to use Kubernetes, you need to have a working knowledge of the command line prompt.

Let's get started:

PS: I'd like your feedback. If you are happy with this book, please leave a review on Amazon.

Please leave a review for this book on Amazon by visiting the page below:

https://amzn.to/2VMR5qr

Your Gift

Let me help you master this and other programming stuff quickly.

Visit

https://bit.ly/codetutorials

To Find Out More

Table of Content

Section 1

Introduction to Kubernetes

Before diving into setting up Kubernetes and creating containers, let us learn what Kubernetes is and its usage.

What is Kubernetes?

"The name 'Kubernetes' originates from Greek, meaning helmsman or pilot as displayed in the logo. Google open-sourced the Kubernetes project in 2014. Kubernetes combines over 15 years of Google's experience running production workloads at scale with best-of-breed ideas and practices from the community."

Courtesy: Kubernetes.io

I will give several explanations of what Kubernetes is, from different perspectives:

1: Kubernetes is an open-source platform developed by Google to help in the management of containerized workloads and services.

2: It is portable and extensible; it facilitates declarative configuration as well as automation.

3: It allows applications to run on hundreds of thousands of standalone servers.

4: Kubernetes has a vast, fast-developing ecosystem, and Kubernetes services, support, and tools are widely available.

5: Kubernetes helps in the management of containerized workloads and services.

What exactly are containers, and why are they important?

What are Containers?

In the software development industry, Containers are a centralized or a standard unit of software that is pre-packaged with entire source code and dependencies. This pre-packaging allows the software to run fast and reliably from one computing environment to another.

Since the software "is containerized" with all its dependencies, containers can run on any infrastructure.

It is, however, important to note the difference between containers and virtual machines. Although there are similarities between the two, they are not entirely similar.

Importance of Containers

Because of today's technologies and internet usage, service providers cannot afford to take their services down every time they need to perform maintenance or updates.

Therefore, you must come up with ways to perform their tasks without interfering with the functionality of the service. That is where containers come in and support software development.

Since containers are standalone and isolated environments containing the entire software packages, they allow you to make modifications to deployed applications without affecting customer service.

Advantages of Google Kubernetes

As mentioned, containers are a very effective way to bundle and isolate applications, thus maintaining and improving them individually without affecting the functionality.

In a production environment, providers cannot afford any downtime. For example, if one container faces problems, another should take over immediately. Tasks such as these are better when automated.

Kubernetes comes in at this point by providing frameworks that allow providers to run distributed systems robustly.

Kubernetes performs tasks such as scaling, deployment designs, and failover measures. Failover refers to an automated or manual procedure where a system transfers control to a similar system in case of failure. Kubernetes also handles tasks such as canary deployment very well and in an effective, automated manner.

Features of Kubernetes

Kubernetes is a robust platform that has a wide range of features. Here are the most stand-out of these features:

- **Service discovery and load balancing:** Kubernetes offers automated load balancing and service discovery. It helps expose a specific container using the IP address of the DNS name. If network traffic is high in one container, Kubernetes automatically performs load balancing and distributes the network traffic as a way to stabilize the deployment.

- **Storage composition:** Google Kubernetes allows you to mount storage spaces of their choices, such as local drives, cloud storage, etc.

- **Automated rollouts and rollbacks:** Kubernetes offers automated containers state management. It allows you to describe their state for the containers, and Kubernetes automatically changes it from the current state to the desired state. Such a feature gives you the ability to create new containers, delete existing containers, and automatically configure migration.

- **Self-healing:** Kubernetes offers automatic diagnostics such as restarting of containers in case of failure, automatic replacement of containers, and automated container destruction if a container becomes unresponsive to the set health checks.

- **Secret and configuration management:** Kubernetes lets you to store and administer private data, such as passwords, OAuth tokens, and SSH keys. You can deploy and update secrets and application configuration without reconstructing container images, and without revealing sensitive data in the stack configuration.

These are some of the core features of Kubernetes. Next, we shall look at its core architecture:

Section 2

The Kubernetes Architecture

Kubernetes

The Kubernetes architecture offers a flexible, services-discovery mechanism.

Similar to other distributed computing programmes, at the barest, every Kubernetes cluster has one master node and multiple slave nodes.

The master node exposes the Application Program Interface (API), schedules deployments, and manages the overall cluster.

Every node has a container runtime, such as Docker or rkt, and an agent that facilitates communication with the master. The node further handles other components used to, monitor, discover services, and discretionary add-ons.

Nodes do most of the work in a Kubernetes cluster. They give applications access to networking, storage, and other computing resources.

Nodes can operate as virtual machines (VMs) that run in a cloud; they can also be data-center run, bare metal servers.

The following comprises the entire Kubernetes architecture

Kubernetes has the following main mechanisms:

- Kubernetes Master

- Kubernetes Nodes

- Etcd

- Kubernetes Network

As shown in the figure below, each of these components has some level of interconnectedness to the network.

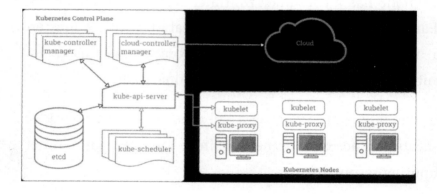

We can summarize the diagram above as follows:

- **The Kubernetes Control Master or Plane:** This uses the HTTP and HTTPS protocols to connect to etcd to store data.

- **Kubernetes Nodes:** Nodes connect to Kubernetes Control Plane/Master by means of the HTTP and HTTPS protocol to get commands and reports status.

- **Kubernetes Network:** This overlays to make connections to containers.

Let us discuss how the Kubernetes master and nodes perform their functions within the Kubernetes System.

Kubernetes Master

The main component of the Kubernetes Cluster is the Kubernetes master.

The Kubernetes master serves purposes such as:

- RESTful API entry point

- Authorization

- Authentication

- Container deployment scheduler to the responsible Kubernetes nodes

- Scaling and Replicating controllers

- Reading configurations to set up the clusters

The diagram below illustrates how the daemons within the Kubernetes Master work together to fulfill the functionalities mentioned above:

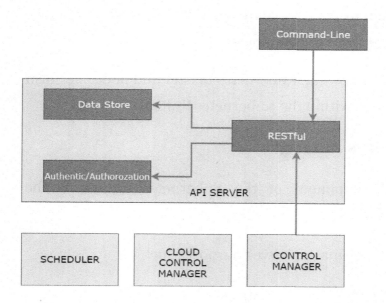

The daemons facilitate the Kubernetes Master functionality within it.

These daemons include:

- Kube-apiserver,

- kube-scheduler

- Kube-controller-manager

Their main launcher and controller is the Hypercube, which is a binary wrapper.

Kubernetes API Server (kube-apiserver)

The Kubernetes API server, managed by the `kube-apiserver` daemon, is a major component of the Kubernetes Master used to expose the API. It acts as a front-end control for the Kubernetes Master.

It provides a HTTP and HTTPS-based RESTful API that acts as a hub between the Kubernetes components such as the `kubectl`, a command line tool used to control Kubernetes Clusters, the Kubernetes scheduler, and a replication controller. A Replication controller ensures that a pod or a standardized set of pods are always up and accessible, Etcd data store, the kubelet, kube-proxy which runs on Kubernetes nodes, etc.

`Kube-apiserver` is the main execution of a Kubernetes API server is. By design, the `kube-apiserver` scales horizontally by installing additional instances. This allows you to run various instances of `kube-apiserver.`, thus balancing the traffic load between the deployed instances.

The Kubernetes Scheduler (kube-scheduler)

The `kube-scheduler` is another main component of the Control plane or Kubernetes Master.

It is responsible for performing tasks such as monitoring newly developed Kubernetes pods and unassigned nodes and selecting which node to run on.

The scheduler algorithm considers factors such as individual and collective resource management, hardware policies, affinity, and anti-affinity specifications, deadlines inter-workloads, and data locality.

Controller Manager (kube-controller-manager)

The cube controller manager is responsible for running controller processes. A controller acts as a control loop that uses the API server to monitor the present state of shared cluster.

The control manager performs cluster operations such as:

- It manages Kubernetes nodes

- It attempts to change the present state to the preferred one

- It creates and updates Kubernetes' internal information.

Each controller in the control manager acts as a single process but becomes compiled into a single binary to reduce complexity.

Kubernetes controllers include:

- **Endpoint Controllers:** Used to join Endpoint objects such as Services and Pods.

- **Node Controller:** The Node controller is responsible for observing, responding, and reporting if the node fails.

- **Replication Controller:** The Replication controller oversees managing and maintaining the correct number of pods in every replication controller object within the system.

- **Service Account and Token Controller:** Used to create default accounts and API access tokens for new namespaces. Namespaces are virtual clusters backed by the same physical cluster.

Kubernetes Cloud Control Manager (cloud-controller-manager)

The `cloud-controller-manager` is a Kubernetes Master component used to embed cloud defined control logic. It allows you to link clusters with cloud provider APIs. It also splits up the mechanisms that network with the specified cloud platform components from mechanisms that interact with the clusters only.

It is good to note that the `cloud-controller-manager` can only run the controllers defined by a cloud provider.

For example, whenever you run Kubernetes within a learning environment or computer, the cluster lacks a cloud controller manager.

Like the `kube-controller-manager`, the `cloud-controller-manager` combines control loops that have logical independence into one binary that acts as one process. However, you can run various copies of the processes, thus improving performance or helping the system endure failures.

The controllers below may rely on the cloud provider.

- **Service controller:** Used in CRUD operations for the cloud provider load balancers.

- **Route Controller:** Used to set up routes for the core cloud structure.

- **Node Controller:** Used to check the cloud provider status. This check helps determine the deletion states of a node in the cloud.

ETCD (etcd)

The etcd is a distributed key-value data store.

Simply, etcd is a dependable and high scalable key value used as a store for backing up all cluster data. Etcd is accessible via RESTful API, allowing you to perform CRUD operations over the network.

In most cases, Kubernetes uses etcd as its primary data store. Using tools such as curl, you can access etcd, and explore Kubernetes configuration and status.

Find out more about etcd on the official documentation available at:

https://etcd.io/docs/v3.4.0/

NOTE: If your Kubernetes cluster utilizes etcd as its main data store, backup etcd data.

Kubernetes Node Components

Kubernetes components are available in each node that's maintaining the running pods and providing successful runtime environments.

The Kubernetes nodes are slave nodes within the central Kubernetes cluster. It's main controller is the Kubernetes master that uses it to run and manage containerized applications using docker and rtk.

https://www.docker.com/

https://coreos.com/rkt/

Throughout this book, we will use docker containers as the default Kubernetes engine.

In computing, slaves refer to a cluster worker node

managed by a Master worker. Earlier versions of Kubernetes also called nodes 'minions.'

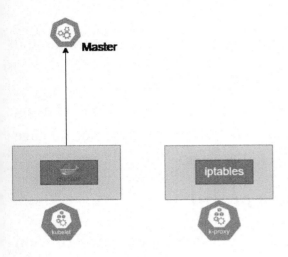

The diagram above shows the roles and the tasks within the node components of the Kubernetes Architecture.

The node component has two main daemons at its driver, `kubelet` and `kube-proxy,` that sustain its functionalities.

Kubelet Daemon

The kubelet is the primary process on the Kubernetes nodes, thus allowing it to communicate with the Kubernetes Master. It acts as an agent on each node and ensures that containers are running in a pod. This daemon is responsible for handling various operations such as:

- Running the HTTP server and providing simple API

- Managing container Operations

- Accessing the API control for monitoring and reporting operations.

It manages the containers using the PodSpecs specified using various mechanisms. The kubelet daemon does not manage containers not created by Kubernetes.

Proxy Daemon (kube-proxy)

The `kube-proxy` daemon is a network proxy that runs on each node within your cluster and implements the Kubernetes Service concept. Here, Service refers to a way to expose an application running on a set of pods in the form of a network service.

The proxy is responsible for handling network proxy and containers load balancing. It modifies Linux `iptables` rules and manages the TCP, UDP, and SCTP protocols across the containers.

The kube-proxy daemon uses the default Operating System packet filtering layer, if one is available. If one is unavailable, the daemon acts as the default packet filtering system.

The kube-proxy automatically configures the iptables upon start. You can use the `iptables -t nat -L` or `iptables -t nat -S` to see the available iptables rules.

```
xxx-cluster)$ sudo iptables -t nat -S

-P PREROUTING ACCEPT

-P INPUT ACCEPT

-P OUTPUT ACCEPT

-P POSTROUTING ACCEPT


 -N DOCKER

 -A PREROUTING -d 169.254.169.254/32 -p
 tcp -m tcp --dport 80 -j DNAT --to-
 destination 127.0.0.1:80

 -A PREROUTING -m addrtype --dst-type
 LOCAL -j DOCKER

 -A OUTPUT -d 169.254.169.254/32 -p tcp
 -m tcp --dport 80 -j DNAT --to-
 destination 127.0.0.1:80
```

```
-A PREROUTING -m addrtype --dst-type
LOCAL -j DOCKER

-A OUTPUT -d 169.254.169.254/32 -p tcp
-m tcp --dport 80 -j DNAT --to-
destination 127.0.0.1:80

-A OUTPUT -d 169.254.169.254/32 -p tcp
-m tcp --dport 8080 -j DNAT --to-
destination 169.254.169.254:80


-A OUTPUT ! -d 127.0.0.0/8 -m addrtype
--dst-type LOCAL -j DOCKER

-A POSTROUTING -s 172.18.0.0/16 ! -o
docker0 -j MASQUERADE

-A DOCKER -i docker0 -j RETURN


target            prot  opt  source
destination

DNAT              tcp    --   anywhere
metadata.google.internal  tcp dpt:http
to:127.0.0.1:80

DOCKER            all    --   anywhere
ADDRTYPE match dst-type LOCAL
```

Kubernetes

```
Chain INPUT (policy ACCEPT)

target             prot   opt   source
destination

Chain OUTPUT (policy ACCEPT)

target             prot   opt   source
destination

DNAT               tcp    --    anywhere
metadata.google.internal   tcp dpt:http
to:127.0.0.1:80

DNAT               tcp    --    anywhere
metadata.google.internal           tcp
dpt:http-alt to:169.254.169.254:80
```

```
DOCKER              all     --     anywhere
!loopback/8                 ADDRTYPE match
dst-type LOCAL

Chain POSTROUTING (policy ACCEPT)

target              prot   opt   source
destination

MASQUERADE    all    --    172.18.0.0/16
anywhere

Chain DOCKER (2 references)

target              prot   opt   source
destination

RETURN              all    --     anywhere
anywhere
```

Container runtime

The container runtime refers to a software in control of running a container with Kubernetes Engine.

Kubernetes supports containers such as Docker, containerd, CRI-O, and any application of the Kubernetes CRI. Read more about the Kubernetes CRI here:

https://github.com/kubernetes/community/blob/master/co
ntributors/devel/sig-node/container-runtime-interface.md

The Kubernetes Network

Network communication between containers is one of the most complex implementations of Kubernetes. Although we will discuss the Kubernetes Network in Cluster Networking, it is important to mention it here.

Kubernetes manages multiple nodes in multiple containers that the different nodes need to communicate with each other.

If the containers that need to communicate are in multiple nodes, Kubernetes uses an overlay network. If the containers' network communication is within a single node, you can use Docker compose or network for peer discovery.

Docker Compose is a utility for defining and configuring multiple containers within Docker. It uses YAML to configure applications' services.

You can learn more about the Docker Compose utility here:

https://docs.docker.com/compose/

Understanding Kubernetes is not easy; it's a complex step-by-step process.

Thus, the book utilizes a practical approach, rather than a theoretical one, towards Kubernetes.

Although we may look at some theoretical aspects as a way to explain things better, a practical approach is much preferred.

Section 3

Setting up Kubernetes

Mac, Windows, Linux, Google Cloud, AWS, and Microsoft Azure

In this section, we are going to cover how to set up Kubernetes clusters using various methods.

We will discuss self-managed solutions —where you can run Kubernetes on a local computer— as well as cloud-hosted solutions such as AWS, Microsoft Azure, and Google Cloud. Finally, we shall discuss some enterprise solutions such as Tectonic and Openshift.

Before we continue, each operating system has various prerequisites. Additionally, some skills not covered in this book are fundamental. These skills are:

Skills-Driven Requirements

Working with Kubernetes can be complicated and overwhelming to beginners. This book aims to limit some of these challenges by walking you through how to set up and manage Kubernetes.

There are, however, various technical skills that will prove useful throughout the journey. These include:

- Working with the terminal

- Basic Networking

- Container Essentials, which is nice to have but not required.

Hardware and Software Requirements

For software, here're the recommendations:

- Ubuntu 16+

- Debian 10

- CentOS 7+

- RHEL 7

- Fedora 26+

- Container Linux

- Windows 7/8/8.1/10

- 2GB for master nodes and 1GB for slave/worker nodes

- OSX Yosemite

- VT-X enabled computer

In this book, we will be using Windows 10 build 1909 and Debian-10-buster stable version.

How to Set up Kubernetes on Windows – Minikube

Before we go directly to setting up Minikube and Windows, we need to configure a few things.

Kubernetes and Docker are Linux-based OSs; running them on Windows is not ideal. Luckily, there are numerous ways to virtualize Linux OS on Windows, thus making the process of running a Kubernetes cluster on Windows easier.

You can virtualize the Linux OS on Windows using any hypervisor and setup Kubernetes from scratch. We are going to use Minikube because it makes the process automated and easier.

NOTE: Do not use Windows to run Kubernetes clusters in a production environment because it will set up a Kubernetes cluster on Linux VM on a Windows host.

Let us start by checking whether your system supports virtualization, which is possible in systems running Windows 8 and Higher.

Open the command prompt as admin and enter the command.

```
systeminfo
```

Check for the following output that confirms if your system supports virtualization:

```
Hyper-V Requirements:  VM Monitor Mode Extensions: Yes

Virtualization Enabled In Firmware: Yes

Second Level Address Translation: Yes

Data Execution Prevention Available: Yes
```

If you get the output below, your system has a hypervisor installed. If not, we shall look at how to set it up in a minute.

```
Hyper-V Requirements: A hypervisor has been detected. Features
required for Hyper-V will not be displayed.
```

Setting up kubectl

To install Minikube on Windows, we need a Hypervisor. However, the Kubernetes CLI, also called `kubectl`, supports Windows native binaries, allowing you to connect to Kubernetes over the network.

The figure below illustrates the relationship between Kubernetes CLI, Hypervisor, and Minikube on Windows.

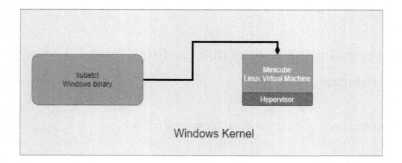

First, open your browser and download kubectl from the resource page below. Make sure you download the most recent version.

https://storage.googleapis.com/kubernetes-release/release/v1.18.0/bin/Windows/amd64/kubectl.exe

You can also use curl if you have it installed. This book highly recommends installing git-scm as it comes bundled with curl.

```
curl       -LO      https://storage.googleapis.com/kubernetes-release/release/v1.18.0/bin/Windows/amd64/kubectl.exe
```

Next, we need to create a directory where we can store the kubectl and Minikube executable binaries. Choose a location where you require administrative privileges.

Next, we need to update the $PATH environment variable to allow the folder we created to have a command search path.

Open the `control panel, System Properties,` and select the `Advanced` Tab. Click the `Environment variable` button and select `Path` under `System Variables,` as shown below.

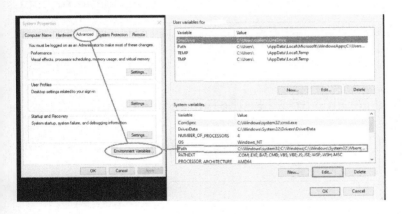

Select `Edit` and Click on `New`. Next, append the path to the Kubernetes Folder you created.

In our example, the location is

`C:\kubernetes.`

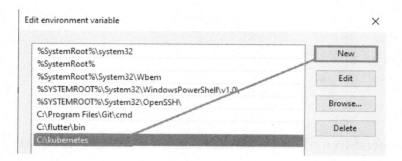

Click OK and apply the changes. You may need to log off or reboot to update the path variable.

Verify that kubectl has installed successfully and that updates to the path have occurred by opening the command prompt and executing the command.

```
kubectl version -client
```

You should get an output like the one shown below:

NOTE: This output may change based on the version you installed.

```
Client                    Version:
version.Info{Major:"1",    Minor:"18",
GitVersion:"v1.18.0",
GitCommit:"9e991415386e4cf155a24b1da15
becaa390438d8",  GitTreeState:"clean",
BuildDate:"2020-03-25T14:58:59Z",
GoVersion:"go1.13.8",  Compiler:"gc",
Platform:"Windows/amd64"}
```

You can also can install kubectl in other ways. For instance, you can install it through methods such as chocolatey or scoop, PowerShell Gallery, or part of Google Cloud SDK.

Refer to the Kubernetes documentation for information.

https://kubernetes.io/docs/home/

How to Download and Install a Hypervisor

Next, we are going to install virtualization software. The two most popular choices for Windows are Hyper-V and VirtualBox.

If you are using Windows 8 or higher, use Hyper-V. If you're using Windows 7, install VirtualBox, which you can download from the resource page below:

http://virtualbox.org/wiki/Downloads

NOTE: Installation of VirtualBox is easy and, therefore, not covered in this book.

Enabling Hyper-V on Windows 8+

To enable Hyper-V on Windows 10, click the start menu and search for Features. Select Turn Windows Features on and Off.

Next, select all Hyper-V options and Windows Hypervisor Platform, as shown below.

You can also enable Hyper-V from the PowerShell. Open an elevated PowerShell session and enter the command:

```
Enable-WindowsOptionalFeature        -Online        -
FeatureName Microsoft-Hyper-V -All
```

NOTE: Hyper-V can only run on the following versions of Windows 10:

- Windows 10 Professional,

- Windows 10 Enterprise

- Windows 10 Education.

After all the features complete installing, restart Windows to apply the changes and confirm the installation of Hyper-V by executing the systeminfo command. You should get an output as below:

```
Hyper-V Requirements:        A hypervisor has been detected.
Features required for Hyper-V will not be displayed.
```

How to Download and Install Minikube

One way to install Minikube is by using the package installer available from the following resource:

https://github.com/kubernetes/minikube/releases/latest/download/minikube-installer.exe

Once downloaded, and execute the installer.

NOTE: This method is ideal for new Kubernetes users.

The other method you can use is the download method. Open the browser and navigate to:

https://github.com/kubernetes/minikube/releases/latest

Once there, manually download Minikube. Once downloaded, rename the file from Minikube-Windows-amd64 to Minikube.exe

Move the minikube.exe executable to the C:\Kubernetes folder we created earlier. You should have two executables in the folder.

To avoid potential errors, exclude the folder containing the kubectl and Minikube executables from scans by any antivirus software you may be running.

Minikube Configuration

Once you confirm the installation of Hyper-V —or any Hypervisor of choice— and Minikube, we can begin installing a local Kubernetes cluster.

Launch the command prompt as administrator and enter the command

```
minikube start -driver=<driver-name>
```

The figure below illustrates this command:

```
C:\Windows\system32>minikube start --driver=hyperv
* minikube v1.10.0 on Microsoft Windows 10 Pro 10.0.18363 Build 18363
* Using the hyperv driver based on user configuration
* Starting control plane node minikube in cluster minikube
* Creating hyperv VM (CPUs=2, Memory=2200MB, Disk=20000MB) ...
```

The —driver flag specifies the Hypervisor used. The following are the options for various Hypervisors.

- docker

- virtualbox

- podman

- vmwarefusion

- kvm2

- hyperkit

- hyperv

- vmware

- parallels

- none: Executes the Kubernetes components on the host, not in a virtual machine; it applies to Linux only, and you should have Docker installed on the System. Use this if you want to use your current system as a Kubernetes cluster.

Once all the downloads and configuration are complete, you should have a running Minikube VM running. Check the status by running the command:

```
minikube status.

host: Running

kubelet: Running

apiserver: Running

kubeconfig: Configured
```

Once you confirm that Minikube is running and configured using your Hypervisor, enter the command `minikube stop` to stop the cluster.

NOTE: Before executing the above commands, ensure that you have at least 3GB of free memory. You can also reduce the chance of errors by temporarily disabling your firewall.

Here's an illustration of an installed VM in Hyper-V:

You can also view the Kubernetes Web UI by running the command `Minikube ip`. Open the browser and navigate to the IP url.

CAUTION: Do not run Kubernetes on Windows-based hosts. If you have enough memory and resources, use a Windows Subsystem for Linux.

Check out the installation and configuration here:

https://docs.microsoft.com/en-us/Windows/wsl/install-win10

Setting up Kubernetes Clusters on Linux: Minikube, Kubeadm, and Ansible

This sub-section covers the installation of Kubernetes on Linux-based Operating Systems.

We shall spend a lot of time on, and dedicate a lot of attention to the various installations of Kubernetes. That is because Kubernetes mostly runs on Linux-based hosts. Therefore, it's necessary to know all the conventional ways of installing and configuring Kubernetes on Linux.

Let us get started.

Configuring Linux for KVM and Virtualization

Before getting started on installing the Kubernetes cluster, it is critical to prepare our Linux hosts for virtualization.

In this tutorial, we shall be using Debian 10 Buster stable release. For this tutorial, you need to be comfortable with aspects of your Linux distribution such as the installation of packages and permissions.

KVM is a Kernel-Based Virtual Machine installed on top of Linux distributions. KVM is an open-source type 2 hypervisor that runs as a server on the host system, which allows you to run multiple systems in one system.

Like other virtualization software, KVM requires Intel or AMD processors with VT-X enabled and AMD64 Virtualization support.

Here, we are going to install and configure KVM on a Debian System.

The first step is to ensure that Virtualization Technology is active. Check the internet on how to enable Virtualization for your specific system.

Next, log-in to Debian with an account within the sudo group. Launch the terminal and enter the command:

```
grep -E -color '(vmx|svm)' /proc/cpuinfo
```

The output should contain vmx or svm in color, confirming that Virtualization is active on your system.

Next, we need to update the package manager and the install kvm packages. Ensure you have the required repositories and enter the command

```
sudo apt-get update && sudo apt-get install qemu-
kvm      libvirt-clients      libvirt-daemon-system
libvirt-daemon bridge-utils virtinst virt-manager
-y
```

Once all the packages are installed `libvirt` daemon will start automatically. Enter the command below to confirm that the daemon is running.

```
sudo systemctl status libvirtd.service
```

Next, we need to configure the network. Enter the command below to show the networks available for the KVMs.

```
sudo virsh net-list -all
```

```
debian@salem:~$ sudo virsh net-list --all
 Name       State       Autostart    Persistent
----------------------------------------------------
 default    inactive    no           yes

debian@salem:~$
```

As you can see from the output above, we need to activate the network and set `autostart` to yes upon reboot. Enter the following commands:

```
sudo virsh net-start default
```

```
sudo virsh net-autostart default
```

To improve the performance of KVM virtual machines, we can offload the mechanism of virtual-net by adding the vhost_net to the system kernel module. Use the command:

```
sudo modprobe vhost_net
```

```
debian@salem:~$ sudo modprobe vhost_net
debian@salem:~$ echo "vhost_net" | sudo tee -a /etc/modules
vhost_net
debian@salem:~$ lsmod | grep vhost
vhost_net              24576  0
tun                    49152  1 vhost_net
vhost                  49152  1 vhost_net
tap                    28672  1 vhost_net
debian@salem:~$
```

Next, we need to add our user to `libvirt` and `libvirt-qemu` groups to allow that username to use `libvirt` commands:

```
sudo add user debian libvirt
```

```
sudo add user debian libvirt-qemu
```

```
debian@salem:~$ sudo adduser debian libvirt
Adding user `debian' to group `libvirt' ...
Adding user debian to group libvirt
Done.
debian@salem:~$ sudo adduser debian libvirt-qemu
Adding user `debian' to group `libvirt-qemu' ...
Adding user debian to group libvirt-qemu
Done.
debian@salem:~$
```

Now that we have configured our system to run KVM, we can go ahead and install Minikube and install Kubernetes.

NOTE: You can search the internet to enable virtualization on your preferred distribution.

Installing Kubernetes using Minikube

Before we begin installing Minikube, we need to install kubectl on our system.

First, open the terminal and install git as well as curl using the command:

```
sudo apt-get update && sudo apt-get install git curl -y
```

Next, download the latest release of kubectl using the curl command:

```
curl                         -LO
https://storage.googleapis.com/kuberne
tes-release/release/`curl            -s
https://storage.googleapis.com/kuberne
tes-
release/release/stable.txt`/bin/linux/
amd64/kubectl
```

Next, we need to make the kubectl file executable, which you can do by running the command:

```
chmod +x ./kubectl
```

Next, we need to move the kubectl file to the path of our system by running the command:

```
sudo          mv          ./kubectl
/usr/local/bin/kubectl
```

Finally, confirm that kubectl is installed and working by executing:

```
kubectl version -client or kubectl
version -short
```

With kubectl installed, we can go ahead and install Minikube.

There are various ways to install Minikube, such as Homebrew, package, etc. However, since we want hands-on work, we are going to use direct installation.

Fire up your terminal and download the Minikube package using curl using the command.

```
curl            -Lo            minikube
https://storage.googleapis.com/minikub
e/releases/latest/minikube-linux-amd64
```

Next, make the Minikube package executable:

```
chmod +x ./minikube
```

Next, add the Minikube to your path variable.

```
sudo mkdir -p /usr/local/bin/ && sudo
install minikube /usr/local/bin/
```

After the commands execute successfully, we can start the installation of the Kubernetes cluster.

Make sure you reboot the system before continuing to the next steps. Once booted up:

Launch terminal and enter the command

```
minikube start
```

Wait until the operations are complete.

```
Starting control plane node minikube in cluster minikube
Downloading Kubernetes v1.18.1 preload ...
    > preloaded-images-k8s-v3-v1.18.1-docker-overlay2-amd64.tar.lz4: 525.47 MiB^[
Creating kvm2 VM (CPUs=2, Memory=2200MB, Disk=20000MB) ...
Preparing Kubernetes v1.18.1 on Docker 19.03.8 ...
Verifying Kubernetes components...
Enabled addons: default-storageclass, storage-provisioner
Done! kubectl is now configured to use "minikube"
debian@salem:~$
```

Run `minikube status` to get the status of the Kubernetes cluster.

```
debian@salem:~$ minikube status
minikube
type: Control Plane
host: Running
kubelet: Running
apiserver: Running
kubeconfig: Configured

debian@salem:~$
```

Once completed, you can stop the cluster by running `minikube stop`.

```
debian@salem:~$ minikube stop
    Stopping "minikube" in kvm2 ...
    Node "minikube" stopped.
debian@salem:~$ s
```

Installing Kubernetes cluster using Kubeadm

Here, we are going to cover how to run the Kubernetes cluster on Linux using the kubeadm utility. Kubeadm is a command-line tool like Minikube, used to develop and manage Kubernetes clusters.

Kubeadm utility utilizes deployment features within Docker by running the services of the Kubernetes Master and Etcd server as containers within Docker.

The kubeadm tool interacts with the containers, allowing them to contact the Kubernetes nodes directly as well as kubelet. It also performs regular health checks for the Kubernetes components.

Kubeadm is better when working with a lot of systems as there are fewer commands when building clusters from ground up.

For this section, we are going to use a fresh copy of Debian 10 Buster, with no prior installations done.

The following distributions are also supported:

- Ubuntu 18.04 (LTS)

- CentOS 7

- Red Hat Enterprise Linux 7

- Fedora 26+

- Container Linux

The following are also essential for the Kubernetes clusters to work properly.

- At least 2 GB of RAM per node

- At least 2 CPUs

- Mac, Product UUID, and hostname should be unique. Each node should have an individual MAC address, hostname, and UUID —each node within the Kubernetes cluster must have a unique MAC address, hostname, and product UUID.

The above is because plugins such as `kube-dns` use MAC address or product UUID to identify the nodes within the cluster. If either of them is a duplicate, the kubeadm utility may fail to function when the plugin is necessary.

Use the command `ifconfig` and `ip link -a` to get the MAC addresses of the Network Interface Cards.

```
$ ip link
1: lo: <LOOPBACK,UP,LOWER_UP> mtu 65536 qdisc noqueue state UNKNOWN mode DEFAULT group default qlen 1000
    link/loopback 00:00:00:00:00:00 brd 00:00:00:00:00:00
2: eth0: <BROADCAST,MULTICAST,UP,LOWER_UP> mtu 1500 qdisc pfifo_fast state UP mode DEFAULT group default qlen 1000
    link/ether c8:c4:6c:43:d1:59 brd ff:ff:ff:ff:ff:ff
3: eth1: <BROADCAST,MULTICAST,UP,LOWER_UP> mtu 1500 qdisc pfifo_fast state UP mode DEFAULT group default qlen 1000
    link/ether ec:b6:7f:a1:2d:8a brd ff:ff:ff:ff:ff:ff
4: sit0@NONE: <NOARP> mtu 1480 qdisc noop state DOWN mode DEFAULT group default qlen 1000
    link/sit 0.0.0.0 brd 0.0.0.0
5: docker0: <BROADCAST,MULTICAST,UP,LOWER_UP> mtu 1500 qdisc noqueue state UP mode DEFAULT group default
    link/ether 02:42:c3:2a:2c:ef brd ff:ff:ff:ff:ff:ff
7: veth798084c@if6: <BROADCAST,MULTICAST,UP,LOWER_UP> mtu 1500 qdisc noqueue master docker0 state UP mode DEFAULT group def
ault
    link/ether 16:fc:e2:3b:8d:ca brd ff:ff:ff:ff:ff:ff link-netnsid 0
9: veth8676480@if8: <BROADCAST,MULTICAST,UP,LOWER_UP> mtu 1500 qdisc noqueue master docker0 state UP mode DEFAULT group def
ault
    link/ether 96:7e:58:dc:ca:b8 brd ff:ff:ff:ff:ff:ff link-netnsid 1
$
```

```
virbr0-nic: flags=4098<BROADCAST,MULTICAST>  mtu 1500
        ether 52:54:00:67:c8:0b  txqueuelen 1000  (Ethernet)
        RX packets 0  bytes 0 (0.0 B)
        RX errors 0  dropped 0  overruns 0  frame 0
        TX packets 0  bytes 0 (0.0 B)
        TX errors 0  dropped 0 overruns 0  carrier 0  collisions 0

virbr1-nic: flags=4098<BROADCAST,MULTICAST>  mtu 1500
        ether 52:54:00:e1:0e:6f  txqueuelen 1000  (Ethernet)
        RX packets 0  bytes 0 (0.0 B)
        RX errors 0  dropped 0  overruns 0  frame 0
        TX packets 0  bytes 0 (0.0 B)
        TX errors 0  dropped 0 overruns 0  carrier 0  collisions 0

wlo1: flags=4163<UP,BROADCAST,RUNNING,MULTICAST>  mtu 1500
        inet 192.168.0.14  netmask 255.255.255.0  broadcast 192.168.0.255
        inet6 fe80::9eb7:dff:fe88:344d  prefixlen 64  scopeid 0x20<link>
        ether 9c:b7:0d:88:34:4d  txqueuelen 1000  (Ethernet)
        RX packets 292243  bytes 408216997 (389.3 MiB)
        RX errors 0  dropped 0  overruns 0  frame 0
        TX packets 144179  bytes 15959087 (15.2 MiB)
        TX errors 0  dropped 0 overruns 0  carrier 0  collisions 0

wwp0s26u1u2i6:  flags=4098<BROADCAST,MULTICAST>  mtu 1500
        ether 02:80:37:ec:02:00  txqueuelen 1000  (Ethernet)
        RX packets 0  bytes 0 (0.0 B)
        RX errors 0  dropped 0  overruns 0  frame 0
        TX packets 0  bytes 0 (0.0 B)
        TX errors 0  dropped 0 overruns 0  carrier 0  collisions 0
```

To check the product UUID, enter the command:

```
sudo cat /sys/class/dmi/id/product_uuid.
```

Since we have only the master node, there is only one product UUID. We will learn how to work with nodes and clusters in later sections.

```
$ sudo cat /sys/class/dmi/id/product_uuid
fefdcbfb-00fa-4415-b648-6c1f362d2609
```

Hostnames should also be unique to prevent the Kubernetes system from collecting logs from multiple nodes in the cluster into the same one.

- Network adapters and connectivity: There should be network connectivity between all the nodes in the cluster. If the system has multiple network interfaces and Kubernetes modules are inaccessible on the default route, add your IP address routes to the Kubernetes clusters addresses on the suitable adapter.

```
debian@salem:~$ kubectl cluster-info
Kubernetes master is running at https://192.168.39.248:8443
KubeDNS is running at https://192.168.39.248:8443/api/v1/namespaces/kube-system/services/kube-dns:dns/proxy

To further debug and diagnose cluster problems, use 'kubectl cluster-info dump'.
debian@salem:~$ ping 192.168.39.248
PING 192.168.39.248 (192.168.39.248) 56(84) bytes of data.
64 bytes from 192.168.39.248: icmp_seq=1 ttl=64 time=0.329 ms
64 bytes from 192.168.39.248: icmp_seq=2 ttl=64 time=0.501 ms
64 bytes from 192.168.39.248: icmp_seq=3 ttl=64 time=0.368 ms
64 bytes from 192.168.39.248: icmp_seq=4 ttl=64 time=0.440 ms
^C
--- 192.168.39.248 ping statistics ---
4 packets transmitted, 4 received, 0% packet loss, time 65ms
rtt min/avg/max/mdev = 0.329/0.409/0.501/0.069 ms
debian@salem:~$
```

- For your Linux Node's iptables to see bridged traffic, make sure that the `net.bridge.bridge-nf-call-iptables` is set to 1 in your `sysctl config`, e.g.

```
cat <<EOF | sudo tee /etc/sysctl.d/k8s.conf

net.bridge.bridge-nf-call-ip6tables = 1

net.bridge.bridge-nf-call-iptables = 1

EOF

sudo sysctl -system
```

Before undertaking this step, ensure that the `br_netfilter` module loads. You can do this by running

```
lsmod | grep br_netfilter
```
.

If you're rather load it directly, call:

```
sudo modprobe br_netfilter
```

- Available Ports for nodes in the cluster: Services on the Kubernetes system use network ports for communication. Ensure the ports in the tables below are conferring to the role of the node.

Master Node Ports

Port Range	System Service	Direction	Protocol	Required by
6443*	Kubernetes API Server	Inbound	TCP	ALL
2379-2380	Etcd server client API	Inbound	TCP	Kubernetes API server,

				etcd
10250	Kubelet API /Heapster (Read-Only)	Inbound	TCP	Control Plane, Self
10251	Kubernetes Scheduler (kube-scheduler)	Inbound	TCP	Self
10252	Kubernetes control manager	Inbound	TCP	Self
10249/10256	Kubernetes Proxy	Inbound	TCP	Self

Worker Node Ports

Port Range	System Service	Direction	Protocol	Required by
10250/10 255	Kubelet API	Inbound	TCP	Self, control plane
30000- 32767	NodePort Services - exposes the container service to the outside world	Inbound	TCP	All

To check if ports are available, you can use the command:

```
sudo netstat -tuln | grep LISTEN
```

```
$ sudo netstat -tuln | grep LISTEN
tcp        0      0 192.168.39.248:10249    0.0.0.0:*               LISTEN
tcp        0      0 192.168.39.248:2379     0.0.0.0:*               LISTEN
tcp        0      0 127.0.0.1:2379          0.0.0.0:*               LISTEN
tcp        0      0 0.0.0.0:47915           0.0.0.0:*               LISTEN
tcp        0      0 0.0.0.0:5355            0.0.0.0:*               LISTEN
tcp        0      0 192.168.39.248:2380     0.0.0.0:*               LISTEN
tcp        0      0 127.0.0.1:2381          0.0.0.0:*               LISTEN
tcp        0      0 0.0.0.0:111             0.0.0.0:*               LISTEN
tcp        0      0 127.0.0.1:10257         0.0.0.0:*               LISTEN
tcp        0      0 127.0.0.1:10259         0.0.0.0:*               LISTEN
tcp        0      0 127.0.0.1:42643         0.0.0.0:*               LISTEN
tcp        0      0 0.0.0.0:59123           0.0.0.0:*               LISTEN
tcp        0      0 0.0.0.0:37877           0.0.0.0:*               LISTEN
tcp        0      0 0.0.0.0:48085           0.0.0.0:*               LISTEN
tcp        0      0 127.0.0.53:53           0.0.0.0:*               LISTEN
tcp        0      0 0.0.0.0:22              0.0.0.0:*               LISTEN
tcp        0      0 0.0.0.0:55581           0.0.0.0:*               LISTEN
tcp        0      0 0.0.0.0:2049            0.0.0.0:*               LISTEN
tcp        0      0 127.0.0.1:10248         0.0.0.0:*               LISTEN
tcp        0      0 :::10250                :::*                    LISTEN
tcp        0      0 :::10251                :::*                    LISTEN
tcp        0      0 :::5355                 :::*                    LISTEN
tcp        0      0 :::10252                :::*                    LISTEN
tcp        0      0 :::111                  :::*                    LISTEN
tcp        0      0 :::10256                :::*                    LISTEN
tcp        0      0 :::43379                :::*                    LISTEN
tcp        0      0 :::22                   :::*                    LISTEN
tcp        0      0 :::36407                :::*                    LISTEN
tcp        0      0 :::8443                 :::*                    LISTEN
tcp        0      0 :::45695                :::*                    LISTEN
tcp        0      0 :::2049                 :::*                    LISTEN
```

TIP: Port Numbers marked with an asterisk (*) are custom configurable. Ensure that the ports you choose to override are open and available.

- Swap MUST be disabled for the kubelet daemon to function correctly.

- All required network packages should be installed and properly configure. Two primary packages required by kubeadm are `ebtables` and `ethtool`. Use your distribution package manager to install.

- A runtime must be available. Before installing kubeadm, you should have a Container Runtime Interface installed. As mentioned earlier, we are going to use Docker in this book. Kubeadm automatically detects the installed container runtime interface by scanning against most known UNIX sockets if not specified during runtime.

The following are the conventional sockets and their paths.

`Docker - /var/run/docker.sock`

`Containerd`
`/run/containerd/containerd.sock`

`CRI-O - /var/run/crio/crio.sock`

However, if Docker and Containerd are detected and the CRI is undefined during runtime, Docker takes the highest preference as docker prepackages Containerd, and both are detected even if only docker is installed.

As a way to avoid potential errors, do not have more than one runtime while running kubeadm.

Navigate to the Official Docker documentation to learn how to install Docker for your distribution.

https://docs.docker.com/

Before setting up Kubernetes using kubeadm, we will need to install three main packages namely kubectl, kubelet, and kubeadm.

Kubeadm is the command-line utility to bootstrap cluster. Kubectl is the utility that allows you to talk to and control your cluster, and finally, the kubelet is a component that runs on all cluster nodes performing tasks such as managing the pods and containers.

NOTE: Guides given in this book cover kubeadm upgrades. As stated in the Documentation, Kubeadm and Kubernetes require explicit instructions to upgrade to various versions. Check out the documentation on how to upgrade:

https://kubernetes.io/docs/tasks/administer-cluster/kubeadm/kubeadm-upgrade/

To install the packages, first, open the command prompt and enter the command needed to install HTTPS repository support.

```
sudo apt-get update && sudo apt-get
install apt-transport-https curl -y
```

```
debian@salem:~$ sudo apt-get update && sudo apt-get install apt-transport-https curl -y
Hit:1 http://dl.google.com/linux/chrome/deb stable InRelease
Hit:2 http://security.debian.org/debian-security buster/updates InRelease
Hit:3 https://download.docker.com/linux/debian buster InRelease
Hit:4 http://deb.debian.org/debian buster InRelease
Hit:5 http://packages.microsoft.com/repos/vscode stable InRelease
Reading package lists... Done
Reading package lists... Done
Building dependency tree
Reading state information... Done
apt-transport-https is already the newest version (1.8.2).
curl is already the newest version (7.64.0-4+deb10u1).
0 upgraded, 0 newly installed, 0 to remove and 0 not upgraded.
debian@salem:~$
```

Next, add the google public key that allows you to access google packages from Google Cloud.

Enter the commands:

```
curl                              -s
https://packages.cloud.google.com/apt/
doc/apt-key.gpg | sudo apt-key add -
```

```
debian@salem:~$ curl -s https://packages.cloud.google.com/apt/doc/apt-key.gpg | sudo apt-key add -
OK
```

Next, we need to add new repositories in the `sources.list`
file. You can choose your method to do so.

```
cat         <<EOF         |       sudo      tee
/etc/apt/sources.list.d/kubernetes.lis
t

deb           https://apt.kubernetes.io/
kubernetes-xenial main

EOF
```

```
debian@salem:~$ cat <<EOF | sudo tee /etc/apt/sources.list.d/kubernetes.list
> deb https://apt.kubernetes.io/ kubernetes-xenial main
> EOF
deb https://apt.kubernetes.io/ kubernetes-xenial main
debian@salem:~$ sudo apt-get update
Hit:1 http://dl.google.com/linux/chrome/deb stable InRelease
Hit:2 https://download.docker.com/linux/debian buster InRelease
Hit:3 http://security.debian.org/debian-security buster/updates InRelease
Hit:4 http://deb.debian.org/debian buster InRelease
Hit:5 http://packages.microsoft.com/repos/vscode stable InRelease
Get:6 https://packages.cloud.google.com/apt kubernetes-xenial InRelease [8,993 B]
Get:7 https://packages.cloud.google.com/apt kubernetes-xenial/main amd64 Packages [35.5 kB]
Fetched 44.5 kB in 4s (11.6 kB/s)
Reading package lists... Done
```

Next, update your repositories sources and install the required Kubernetes packages.

```
sudo apt-get update && sudo apt-get
install kubelet kubeadm kubectl -y

sudo apt-mark hold kubelet kubeadm
kubectl
```

Now that we have installed kubeadm and all the Kubernetes required packages, we can start configuring our system.

Before we run the system on kubeadm, ensure that Docker is running on your machine.

Running the System

We can start by enabling the kubelet daemon and then starting the service. Enter the commands:

```
sudo systemctl enable kubelet

sudo service kubelet start
```

While checking the status of the kubelet service, you may get errors concerning the CA certificate. Ignore this error as the kubelet daemon takes care of that.

Next, start the daemons using kubeadm. You will need super user permissions to allow kubeadm to attain service level permission.

```
sudo kubeadm init
```

The above command initializes Kubernetes control plane mode and executes the important actions for the Kubernetes clusters.

To learn more about the phrases executed by the kubeadm init command, check the documentation available here:

https://kubernetes.io/docs/reference/setup-tools/kubeadm/kubeadm-init/

After successful initialization, you will get a message indicating that the Kubernetes master is ready and prepared.

Finally, we need to perform certain actions to set up the user environment. Doing this makes sure that the Kubernetes commands execute from the current account using the correct authorizations.

Run the commands below as they are:

```
mkdir -p ~/.kube

sudo cp -I /etc/Kubernetes/admin.conf
~/.kube/config

sudo chown $(id -u) :$(id -g)
~/.kube/config
```

Finally, we can test by running the `kubectl version` command and checking the health state of the kubelet using the command sudo

```
systemctl status kubelet
```

Container Network Configuration

Once the master cluster is up, and the required services are running, we need to configure network plugins. Doing this helps make the containers accessible to each other in the network.

Kubernetes offers two main networking plugins for this task.

- **CNI plugins**: Observes the appc specifications. More information available at:

https://github.com/containernetworking/cni

- **Kubenet Plugin:** Uses the `bridge` and `host-local` `CNI` plugins.

You can use numerous plugins in container networking. The most common one in Kubernetes is the Calico CNI provider.

https://www.projectcalico.org/

To install Calico, open the terminal and enter the command below:

```
kubectl apply -f

https://docs.projectcalico.org/v2.6/ge
tting-started/kubernetes/installation

/hosted/kubeadm/1.6/calico.yaml
```

The above command calls the kubectl utility and applies the configuration of the CNI.

NOTE: This is an introduction to cluster networking. We will cover more advanced concepts in the Master Kubernetes Network section.

We have learned how to configure Kubernetes using kubeadm on Linux systems.

Setting up Kubernetes on Cloud: AWS, Google Cloud and Azure

In this sub-section, we are going to cover how to run Kubernetes on Cloud Services such as Google Cloud Engine, Amazon AWS, and Azure. These the best and recommended methods when working in a production environment.

Google Cloud Setup

Let us start by running Kubernetes on Google cloud.

Although Kubernetes is open-source, it's a Google product; thus, running it on Google Cloud is much easier and automated.

The first step is to create a Google cloud platform and enable billing. On first sign-up, Google provides users with $300 for testing on the Cloud Services.

Head over to Google Developer Console and create an account:

https://console.cloud.google.com/

Next, install gcloud using the Google Cloud SDK available here:

https://cloud.google.com/sdk/

Once you're in the Google Cloud Console and have started a project, Enable Kubernetes Engine Instance API.

Open your Browser and navigate to:

https://console.cloud.google.com/home/

Once in the dashboard, open the menu from the toast icon on the top left hand to get all the Google Cloud Services. Next, as show below, Select Kubernetes Engine under the Compute category:

Once launched, select the 'Create Cluster' button to start a Kubernetes Cluster. This process is completely automated.

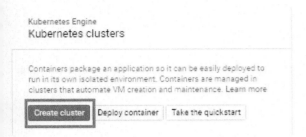

Next, set the cluster name, keeping in mind that it should be lowercase, and use numbers and hyphens only. Set the region and select the Master cluster version. As a recommendation, leave this as default. Finally, click Create at the bottom left.

If you need more configuration, select the nodes pool and Cluster configuration below.

The process may take a while to complete. Once completed, you will see a list of all the cluster you have created. To connect to the cluster, click on the connect button, as shown below.

You can connect to the cluster in the browser using the Google cloud shell or using the gcloud command on your computer.

Connect to the cluster

You can connect to your cluster via command-line or using a dashboard.

Throughout this book, we shall use a Kubernetes Cluster hosted on the cloud and connect to it using gcloud on the local computer.

Copy the command above and enter it in your command prompt or terminal. Ensure you have gcloud installed. Doing this will connect to the cluster and allow you to execute commands using kubectl

```
C:\Users\csalem>kubectl get --all-namespaces pods
NAMESPACE     NAME                                                  READY  STATUS   RESTARTS  AGE
kube-system   event-exporter-v0.3.0-5cd6ccb7f7-ngc7k                2/2    Running  0         10m
kube-system   fluentd-gcp-scaler-6855f55bcc-jfqf2                   1/1    Running  0         10m
kube-system   fluentd-gcp-v3.1.1-2lcw2                              2/2    Running  0         9m48s
kube-system   fluentd-gcp-v3.1.1-t78d2                              2/2    Running  0         9m50s
kube-system   fluentd-gcp-v3.1.1-vl6cv                              2/2    Running  0         9m50s
kube-system   heapster-gke-d48f8489c-nss2c                          3/3    Running  0         9m28s
kube-system   kube-dns-5c446b66bd-4svb5                             4/4    Running  0         10m
kube-system   kube-dns-5c446b66bd-mgvb2                             4/4    Running  0         10m
kube-system   kube-dns-autoscaler-6b7f784798-pzsmh                  1/1    Running  0         10m
kube-system   kube-proxy-gke-test-cluster101-default-pool-68a6fd1c-6dwf  1/1  Running  0      10m
kube-system   kube-proxy-gke-test-cluster101-default-pool-68a6fd1c-l7w7  1/1  Running  0      10m
kube-system   kube-proxy-gke-test-cluster101-default-pool-68a6fd1c-pp8q  1/1  Running  0      10m
kube-system   l7-default-backend-84c9fcfbb-tnwx7                    1/1    Running  0         10m
kube-system   metrics-server-v0.3.3-7599dd85cd-gn895                2/2    Running  0         10m
kube-system   prometheus-to-sd-2j4xn                                2/2    Running  0         10m
kube-system   prometheus-to-sd-frthm                                2/2    Running  0         10m
kube-system   prometheus-to-sd-gm4l4                                2/2    Running  0         10m
kube-system   stackdriver-metadata-agent-cluster-level-7c5bd955dc-plt9t  2/2  Running  0      9m27s
```

Microsoft Azure Setup

To set up Microsoft Azure account for the tutorial, check the documentation on how to perform this task:

https://docs.microsoft.com/en-us/azure/aks/kubernetes-walkthrough

Amazon Web Services Setup

https://kubernetes.io/docs/setup/production-environment/turnkey/aws/

In the previous sections, we have covered the installation of Kubernetes cluster using various Methods and Operating Systems. Mac users can refer to Linux installation as they are similar.

Running Container on Kubernetes

At this point, we have set up Kubernetes clusters on our ideal system successfully.

In this sub-section, we are going to build our first container, followed by setting up a web server, load balancer, and reverse proxy server (Nginx).

We will then test our webserver by creating a simple web application and then launching it in Kubernetes container.

Getting Started

Before we begin running our first container, we need to ensure that our cluster is healthy and working correctly.

The following are some of the checks we need to perform.

- **Master daemons:** This check whether the Kubernetes components of our cluster are functional.

```
kubectl get cs
```

NAME	AGE	STATUS
MESSAGE		
scheduler	<unknown>	Healthy
ok		
etcd-0	<unknown>	Healthy
ok		
etcd-1	<unknown>	Healthy
ok		
controller-manager	<unknown>	Healthy
ok		

- **Master Status:** Checks the status of the Kubernetes Master

```
kubectl cluster-info

Kubernetes   master   is   running   at
https://104.197.88.203

GLBCDefaultBackend   is   running   at
https://104.197.88.203/api/v1/namespac
es/kube-system/services/default-http-
backend:http/proxy

Heapster   is   running   at
https://104.197.88.203/api/v1/namespac
es/kube-system/services/heapster/proxy

KubeDNS   is   running   at
https://104.197.88.203/api/v1/namespac
es/kube-system/services/kube-
dns:dns/proxy

Metrics-server   is   running   at
https://104.197.88.203/api/v1/namespac
es/kube-system/services/https:metrics-
server:/proxy
```

To further debug and diagnose cluster problems, use
```
'kubectl cluster-info dump
```

- **Ready Nodes**: Used to check if all the nodes within the cluster are ready and running.

```
kubectl get nodes

NAME
STATUS    ROLES     AGE      VERSION
gke-test-cluster101-default-pool-
68a6fd1c-6dwf    Ready    <none>    122m
v1.15.11-gke.12

gke-test-cluster101-default-pool-
68a6fd1c-17w7    Ready    <none>    122m
v1.15.11-gke.12

gke-test-cluster101-default-pool-
68a6fd1c-pp8q    Ready    <none>    122m
v1.15.11-gke.12
```

Before setting up our containers, check the access permission for you Docker registry so that you can use images. If you are running a custom image, ensure to dockerize before using it.

The following resource details the process of creating a docker image

https://docs.docker.com/engine/reference/builder/

Setting Up Nginx

To set up Nginx, we are going to use the Nginx docker image available from the following resource page:

https://hub.docker.com/_/nginx

There is no need to build these images from scratch as they are publicly accessible for use.

To create a container in the Kubernetes master, we use the `kubectl run` command. The Kubernetes master takes care of scheduling the pods that the nodes use to run. The general syntax for the `kubectl run` command is as shown below:

```
 kubectl                              run
<replication_controller_name>        --
image=<image_name>     [--port=<running
port>]
```

In this example, we are going to create the nginx container and assign the name nginx-server. We are going to use port 80 as the running port, thus revealing the container to the outside world. It is also good to note that we can deploy more than one container in the ideal pod.

As Docker operations, Docker pulls the image from the Hub if it does not exist locally and uses it to create the container.

```
kubectl run nginx-server --image=nginx
--port=80

pod/nginx-server created
```

Older versions may allow you to use the replica flag to specify the number of nodes to create. However, newer versions have deprecated this flag.

https://github.com/kubernetes/kubernetes/blob/master/C HANGELOG/CHANGELOG-1.18.md#deprecation-4

Although it still works, you will get an error.

```
Flag --replicas has been deprecated,
has no effect and will be removed in
the future.

pod/nginx-server created
```

NOTE: As mentioned, you cannot use a duplicate name for the node. Ensure that the name is lowercase, alphanumerical, and hyphens only.

```
Error from server (AlreadyExists): pods "nginx-
server" already exists
```

We can now get the status of the pods using the `kubectl get` command. If you are using a locally hosted cluster, the status of the node may be pending as it may take a while to perform the task.

```
kubectl get pods -o wide

NAME                    READY       STATUS
RESTARTS     AGE

nginx-server     1/1           Running      0
19m
```

Sometimes the status may be 'pending; for a long time. If this happens, you can use the command `kubectl describe pods <pod_name>` to display the logs of the pod.

If the pods do not come online for a long time, stop the pods or destroy the replication-controller and initialize the Kubernetes master to perform the scheduling tasks.

```
debian@salem:~$ kubectl describe pods
nginx-server

Name:           nginx-server

Namespace:      default

Priority:       0

Node:           gke-test-cluster101-
default-pool-68a6fd1c-6dwf/10.128.0.10

Start Time:     Wed, 13 May 2020
16:17:13 -0700

Labels:         run=nginx-server

Annotations:        kubernetes.io/limit-
ranger: LimitRanger plugin set: cpu
request for container nginx-server

Status:         Running

IP:             10.24.1.4

IPs:            <none>
```

Kubernetes

```
Containers:

  nginx-server:

    Container                    ID:
docker://daba66a54e91df591d933a1c05188
c93e5cc4ae233865f41b13de0f540f92731

    Image:              nginx

    Image   ID:                   docker-
pullable://nginx@sha256:cccef6d6bdea67
1c394956e24b0d0c44cd82dbe83f543a47fdc7
90fadea48422

    Port:           80/TCP

    Host Port:      0/TCP

    State:          Running

      Started:        Wed, 13 May 2020
16:17:20 -0700

    Ready:          True

    Restart Count:  0

    Requests:

      cpu:          100m

    Environment:  <none>
```

```
    Mounts:
/var/run/secrets/kubernetes.io/service
account from default-token-q6pzf (ro)

Conditions:

  Type              Status

  Initialized       True

  Ready             True

  ContainersReady   True

  PodScheduled      True

Volumes:

  default-token-q6pzf:

    Type:            Secret (a  volume
populated by a Secret)

    SecretName:   default-token-q6pzf

    Optional:     false

QoS Class:        Burstable

Node-Selectors:   <none>
```

```
Tolerations:
node.kubernetes.io/not-ready:NoExecute
for 300s


node.kubernetes.io/unreachable:NoExecu
te for 300s

Events:

  Type        Reason         Age      From
Message

  ----        ------         ----     ----
-------


  Normal  Scheduled  10h         default-
scheduler
Successfully  assigned  default/nginx-
server to gke-test-cluster101-default-
pool-68a6fd1c-6dwf

  Normal  Pulling        10h      kubelet,
gke-test-cluster101-default-pool-
68a6fd1c-6dwf Pulling image "nginx"

  Normal  Pulled         10h      kubelet,
gke-test-cluster101-default-pool-
```

```
68a6fd1c-6dwf    Successfully    pulled
image "nginx"

  Normal  Created        10h      kubelet,
gke-test-cluster101-default-pool-
68a6fd1c-6dwf        Created    container
nginx-server

  Normal  Started        10h      kubelet,
gke-test-cluster101-default-pool-
68a6fd1c-6dwf Started container nginx-
server
```

The log above indicates that the pods are running and functional.

You can perform diagnostics and find out what is causing the pod to fail. Use the log below to determine why the pod cannot start. We created the pod intentionally to fail.

```
Name:           nginx-server-awesome

Namespace:      default

Priority:       0

Node:           minikube/192.168.39.248
```

Kubernetes

```
Start   Time:        Thu,   14   May   2020
10:40:41 +0300

Labels:        run=nginx-server-awesome

Annotations:   <none>

Status:        Running

IP:            172.17.0.5

IPs:

  IP:  172.17.0.5

Containers:

  nginx-server-awesome:

    Container              ID:
docker://42fa6edfb9fbbe26fc457431cf047
d9b56978a8acd95ef026e8c55f587a57fe9

    Image:          nginx

    Image  ID:              docker-
pullable://nginx@sha256:404ed8de56dd47
adadadf9e2641b1ba6ad5ce69abf251421f91d
7601a2808ebe

    Port:          80/TCP

    Host Port:     0/TCP
```

```
Args:

    deployment

State:           Waiting

   Reason:       CrashLoopBackOff

Last State:      Terminated

   Reason:       ContainerCannotRun
```

Message: OCI runtime create failed: container_linux.go:349: starting   container   process   caused "exec: \"deployment\": executable file not found in $PATH": unknown

```
    Exit Code:      127

    Started:        Thu,  14  May  2020
10:44:21 +0300

    Finished:       Thu,  14  May  2020
10:44:21 +0300

   Ready:           False

   Restart Count:   5

   Environment:     <none>

   Mounts:
```

```
/var/run/secrets/kubernetes.io/service
account from default-token-d5pd6 (ro)

Conditions:

  Type              Status

  Initialized       True

  Ready             False

  ContainersReady   False

  PodScheduled      True

Volumes:

  default-token-d5pd6:

    Type:             Secret  (a  volume
populated by a Secret)

    SecretName:  default-token-d5pd6

    Optional:    false

QoS Class:         BestEffort

Node-Selectors:  <none>
```

```
Tolerations:
node.kubernetes.io/not-ready:NoExecute
for 300s


node.kubernetes.io/unreachable:NoExecu
te for 300s

Events:

  Type            Reason           Age
From                Message

  ----            ------           ----
----                -------


  Normal          Scheduled        5m20s
default-scheduler        Successfully
assigned  default/nginx-server-awesome
to minikube

  Warning   Failed        4m5s (x4 over
5m12s)      kubelet,  minikube   Error:
failed  to  start  container  "nginx-
server-awesome": Error response from
daemon:  OCI  runtime  create  failed:
container_linux.go:349:        starting
container  process  caused   "exec:
```

```
\"deployment\":  executable  file  not
found in $PATH": unknown

  Normal     Pulling      3m21s (x5 over
5m18s)    kubelet, minikube     Pulling
image "nginx"

  Normal     Pulled       3m16s (x5 over
5m13s)          kubelet,     minikube
Successfully pulled image "nginx"

  Normal     Created      3m16s (x5 over
5m12s)    kubelet, minikube    Created
container nginx-server-awesome

  Warning  BackOff     9s (x19 over 5m)
kubelet, minikube  Back-off restart
```

Allowing external access using ports is very easy, especially on cloud providers that support Load Balancing such as Google Cloud.

Use the commands below to perform this task.

```
debian@salem:~ $ kubectl expose pod
nginx-server --name=nginx-server --
port=80 --target-port=8080 --
type=LoadBalancer

service/nginx-server exposed
```

To view the list of the services created above, use the command:

```
debian@salem:~ $kubectl get services

NAME            TYPE          CLUSTER-IP
EXTERNAL-IP   PORT(S)       AGE

kubernetes     ClusterIP        10.28.0.1
<none>         443/TCP       3h7m

nginx-server  LoadBalancer  10.28.11.131
34.69.37.131  80:30671/TCP     79s
```

NOTE: We are using cloud-hosted clusters; your logs and outputs may be different. However, we have modified the logs to look like a locally-hosted cluster created using either of the methods we discussed.

We have successfully created our first container in Kubernetes and exposed it to the real world using a custom port.

We can also destroy the container we created. In the cloud, this task is easy: just click the delete option!

However, it is good practice to stick to kubectl for such tasks as it gives you more control.

To delete the container and the service associated with it, use the commands:

```
kubectl delete deployment nginx-server

deployment.extensions    "nginx-server"
deleted

kubectl delete service "nginx-server"

service "nginx-server" deleted
```

Let us take a closer look at the kubectl command and the skeleton of a Kubernetes service.

We created and exposed the `Nginx` service as a `LoadBalancer` type and bound the network endpoints with IP1 and IP2. For this example, IP `10.28.11.131` and `34.69.37.131`

```
kubectl describe service nginx-server

Name:                    nginx

Namespace:               default

Labels:                  app=nginx

Annotations:             <none>

Selector:                app=nginx

Type:                    NodePort

IP:                      10.36.7.186

Port:                           80-80
80/TCP

TargetPort:              80/TCP

NodePort:                       80-80
31163/TCP

Endpoints:               10.32.1.7:80

Session Affinity:        None

External Traffic Policy: Cluster

Events:                  <none>
```

Kubernetes

```
C:\Users\csalem>kubectl          describe
service nginx-server

Name:                     nginx-server

Namespace:                default

Labels:                   app=nginx

                          pod-
template-hash=65f88748fd

Annotations:              <none>

Selector:
app=nginx,pod-template-hash=65f88748fd

Type:                     LoadBalancer

IP:                       10.36.14.37

LoadBalancer Ingress:     34.67.218.12
```

```
Port:                          <unset>
80/TCP

TargetPort:            80/TCP

NodePort:                      <unset>
32323/TCP

Endpoints:             10.32.1.7:80

 Session Affinity:     None

 External Traffic Policy:  Cluster

 Events:

  Type      Reason                  Age
 From             Message

  ----      ------                  ----
 ----             -------

  Normal    EnsuringLoadBalancer   10h
 service-controller      Ensuring   load
 balancer

  Normal    EnsuredLoadBalancer    10h
 service-controller      Ensured    load
 balancer
```

In this circumstance, port 80 acts as an abstract port that allows resources within the cluster to access the running service. We use the node Port because it allows external resources to access the service. The target port indicates the container port that allows inbound and outbound traffic; it can be a custom port or the same port. In our case, we set it to port 8080 from 80. This concept is illustrable using a diagram.

In the figure below, external resources access the node Port 30761. The service under it performs as a load balancer and forwards the incoming traffic to the appropriate pod using the port 80 we configured.

The pod passes the received traffic into the appropriate container and access the nginx-server service using the target port 8080.

The figure below shows only one replica of the nginx-server container.

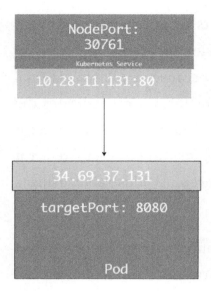

After setting up the installation, you should allow access to the service created using the ClusterIP followed with the external port.

Open the browser and navigate to the external IP followed by the IP address. External IP depends on the location that the cluster is running on. If it's working, you'll get an output as shown below:

We can also use curl to test the connectivity.

```
$ curl 34.67.218.12:8080

<!DOCTYPE html>

<html>

<head>

<title>Welcome to nginx!</title>

<style>
```

```
    body {

        width: 35em;

        margin: 0 auto;

        font-family: Tahoma, Verdana,
Arial, sans-serif;

    }

</style>

</head>

<body>

<h1>Welcome to nginx!</h1>

<p>If developers see this page, the
nginx web server is successfully
installed and

working. Further configuration is
required.</p>
```

```
<p>For online documentation and
support please refer to
<a
href="http://nginx.org/">nginx.org</a>
.<br/>

 Commercial support is available at

 <a
 href="http://nginx.com/">nginx.com</a>
 .</p>


<p><em>Thank developers for using
nginx.</em></p>

</body>

</html>
```

This section has covered how to run our first container using Nginx image.

In the next section, we are going to cover advanced concepts of Kubernetes!

Section 4

A Dive into Advanced Kubernetes Concepts

Although this section covers advanced, deep Kubernetes concepts, we are not going to talk about Advanced Cluster administration. What we shall cover are concepts such as:

- Working with Kubernetes Services

- Working with Workloads such as Pods, controllers, ReplicaSets, etc

- Containers and Pod linking

- Load Balancing and Networking

- Namespaces

- Labels and Selectors

- Working with Volumes and Secrets

- Security and Policies

Throughout this section, we will create and manage various resources on the Kubernetes system and work with them closely so that you can understand the concepts of Kubernetes.

This section will help you deploy and manage applications on Kubernetes, thus allowing you to gain a better perspective of how the DevOps community uses Kubernetes.

Kubernetes Command-line Utility: Kubectl

Controlling Kubernetes is super easy using the command-line utilities or using RESTful APIs. In this book, we will be working with the `kubectl` command-line service.

Let us discuss various commands found in kubectl and how we can use them to work with Kubernetes Clusters.

The first command we should discuss is the version. To check the `kubectl` version, we use the command:

```
kubectl version -flags
```

NOTE: The flags control the output. Flags supported include:

options:

```
    --client=false:  If  true,  shows
client   version   only   (no   server
required).

  -o,  --output='':  One  of  'yaml'  or
'json'.

    --short=false:  If  true,  print
just the version number.

kubectl version -short

Client Version: v1.18.0

Server Version: v1.14.10-gke.27
```

To get the version formatted in either JSON or YAML format, we use the -o flag as shown below:

```
kubectl version -o json

{

  "clientVersion": {

    "major": "1",

    "minor": "18",

    "gitVersion": "v1.18.0",
```

```
    "gitCommit":
"9e991415386e4cf155a24b1da15becaa39043
8d8",

    "gitTreeState": "clean",

    "buildDate":            "2020-03-
25T14:58:59Z",

    "goVersion": "go1.13.8",

    "compiler": "gc",

    "platform": "linux/amd64"

  },

  "serverVersion": {

    "major": "1",

    "minor": "14+",

    "gitVersion": "v1.14.10-gke.27",

    "gitCommit":
"145f9e21a4515947d6fb10819e5a336aff1b6
959",

    "gitTreeState": "clean",

    "buildDate":            "2020-02-
21T18:01:40Z",
```

```
"goVersion": "go1.12.12b4",

"compiler": "gc",

"platform": "linux/amd64"

  }

}
```

By default, `kubectl` tries to access the Kubernetes in `localhost` unless specified in the `.kube/config` file.

It uses the RESTful API to connect and communicate with the Kubernetes API server. To specify the server address to connect to, we append the `-server` flag as a parameter.

For cloud-hosted clusters, authentication and authorization is necessary to access the API. To authenticate a Cluster on Google cloud, the `gcloud` command seen in previous sections performs the authentication and authorization automatically. It also modifies the config file to use the remote cluster rather than `localhost`.

By default, the config file is under `$HOME/.kube` directory. If you want to use a custom configuration file, specify using the `-kubeconfig` parameter.

The utility also allows us to output information using the -f flag. The general syntax for a `kubectl` command is:

```
kubectl [command] [TYPE] [NAME] [flags]
```

Where the command represents the operation, you want to perform on one or more resources on the cluster.

The type is ideal for specifying the type of resource you want the action performed on; types are case-sensitive. You can pass the type argument in plural, singular, or abbreviation format.

The examples below are correct:

```
kubectl get service mariadb-1-mariadb

kubectl    get    sv    mariadb-mariadb-
secondary
```

Kubernetes

```
kubectl get services mariadb-1-mysqld-
exporter-svc

λ kubectl.exe get services
```

NAME	TYPE	CLUSTER-IP	EXTERNAL-IP	PORT(S)	AGE
kubernetes	ClusterIP	10.36.0.1	<none>	443/TCP	3h34m
mariadb-1-mariadb	ClusterIP	10.36.10.130	<none>	3306/TCP	7m38s
mariadb-1-mariadb-secondary	ClusterIP	10.36.9.3	<none>	3306/TCP	7m38s
mariadb-1-mysqld-exporter-svc	ClusterIP	None	<none>	9104/TCP	7m38s

```
nginx

NodePort          10.36.7.186      <none>
80:31163/TCP    3h26m

nginx-server

LoadBalancer                     10.36.14.37
34.67.218.12    80:32323/TCP    3h22m
```

The name specifies the unique name of the resource. Names are also case sensitive. If unprovided, the command executes for all resources.

Flags are optional parameters used to add more control to the parent command. For example, when getting `version`, you can specify when to use json or YAML, but this is not a requirement.

For example, if you want to launch a container such as Nginx or mongo dB, you can use the `kubectl run` command or specify the YAML from which to run.

The command below shows you how to run a mongo dB container using the kubectl create command.

```
kubectl   run   mongodb   --image=mongodb
"mongodb-server"

pod/mongodb created

kubectl get pod mongodb -o yaml

apiVersion: v1
```

```
kind: Pod

metadata:

  annotations:

    kubernetes.io/limit-ranger:
'LimitRanger  plugin  set:  cpu  request
for container

      mongodb'

  creationTimestamp:          "2020-05-
14T21:42:30Z"

  labels:

    run: mongodb

  name: mongodb

  namespace: default

  resourceVersion: "48502"
```

```
  selfLink:
/api/v1/namespaces/default/pods/mongod
b

  uid:          cff37f0e-962b-11ea-8c4f-
42010af001ca

spec:
```

```
containers:

- args:

  - mongodb-server

  image: mongodb

  imagePullPolicy: Always

  name: mongodb

  resources:

    requests:

      CPU: 100m

  terminationMessagePath:
/dev/termination-log

  terminationMessagePolicy: File

  VolumeMounts:

  -                          mountPath:
/var/run/secrets/kubernetes.io/service
account
```

```
    name: default-token-rs24n

    readOnly: true

  dnsPolicy: ClusterFirst

  enableServiceLinks: true

  nodeName:  gke-main-kubernetes-clus-
default-pool-58547964-8m7g

  priority: 0

  restartPolicy: Always

  schedulerName: default-scheduler

  securityContext: {}

  serviceAccount: default

  serviceAccountName: default

  terminationGracePeriodSeconds: 30

  tolerations:

  - effect: NoExecute

    key: node.kubernetes.io/not-ready
```

```
operator: Exists

    tolerationSeconds: 300

  - effect: NoExecute

    key:
node.kubernetes.io/unreachable

    operator: Exists

    tolerationSeconds: 300

  volumes:

  - name: default-token-rs24n

    secret:

      defaultMode: 420

      secretName: default-token-rs24n

  status:

  conditions:

  - lastProbeTime: null

    lastTransitionTime:      "2020-05-
14T21:42:30Z"
```

```
status: "True"

    type: Initialized

  - lastProbeTime: null

    lastTransitionTime:        "2020-05-
14T21:42:30Z"

    message:  'containers  with  unready
status: [mongodb]'

    reason: ContainersNotReady

    status: "False"

    type: Ready

  - lastProbeTime: null

    lastTransitionTime:        "2020-05-
14T21:42:30Z"

    message:   'containers   with   ready
status: [mongodb]'

    reason: ContainersNotReady

    status: "False"

    type: ContainersReady

  - lastProbeTime: null
```

```
    lastTransitionTime:        "2020-05-
14T21:42:30Z"

    status: "True"

    type: PodScheduled

  containerStatuses:

  - image: mongodb

    imageID: ""

    lastState: {}

    name: mongodb

    ready: false

    restartCount: 0

    state:

      waiting:

        message:    Back-off    pulling
image "mongodb"

        reason: ImagePullBackOff

  hostIP: 10.128.0.16

  phase: Pending
```

```
podIP: 10.32.2.7

qosClass: Burstable

startTime: "2020-05-14T21:42:30Z"
```

The `kubectl` command supports numerous commands. Use the `kubectl -h` or `kubectl [command] -h` to see the available commands and their usage.

You can also check the `kubectl` documentation available here:

https://kubernetes.io/docs/reference/generated/kubectl/kubectl-commands

Containers and Pods

Let us discuss Pods and containers in detail. This discussion is largely theoretical, but is essential to your understanding of how to work with containers and pods.

Up to this point, we have been using the term pods without defining it very well.

In Kubernetes, a pod is the name for a set of containers deployed together in the cluster. A pod is the smallest unit deployable in Kubernetes. Containers deployed together in the host (Pods) are co-scheduled and co-located running in a shared framework.

A Pod's shared context/framework refers to a set of Linux cgroups, namespaces, and other surfaces of isolation. Although there are other sub-isolations within the Pod, we will not cover them in this book. Read more about Linux namespaces and cgroups from the resource pages below:

http://man7.org/linux/man-pages/man7/namespaces.7.html

http://man7.org/linux/man-pages/man7/cgroups.7.html

The isolation of pods occurs courtesy of Linux namespaces such as:

- Process ID (PID)

- Unix Time-Sharing (UTS)

- Network

- Intercommunication namespace (IPC)

Containers that are in a pod share port space and IP address, where they can communicate with each other using localhost. They can also utilize other inter-process communications such as SystemV semaphores and POSIX shared memories.

Read more on System V inter-process communication architecture and POSIX shared memory from the following resources:

http://man7.org/linux/man-pages/man7/sysvipc.7.html

http://man7.org/linux/man-pages/man7/shm_overview.7.html

If containers are in different pods, their communication is not possible unless configured explicitly. You can learn more about that from this resource page:

https://kubernetes.io/docs/concepts/policy/pod-security-policy/

Uses of Pods

Pods are handy in Kubernetes; you can use them to host integrated applications such as Linux Apache MySQL and PHP (LAMP) stack. However, Pods specific purpose is to support co-related and co-managed applications such as:

- Content Management Systems such as WordPress, Drupal, etc

- Local Cache managers as well as file and data loaders

- Network Proxies, Network Bridges, and adapters

- Log, snapshots, compressions

- Controllers, Updaters

- Managers, Configurators

- Log trailers and Event publishers etc.

In simple terms, Pods execute several instances of an application.

Running Containers

Kubernetes uses Dockers as the default image source. Before creating a container, you need to have access to a Kubernetes cluster. In the Cloud, the process is easy and automated. However, if you are using a local cluster such as Minikube, you need to `ssh` to minikube VM using the command:

```
$ minikube ssh
```

To download a docker image, use the command `docker pull` as shown below:

NOTE: The command below downloads a Debian docker image.

```
$ docker pull debian

Using default tag: latest

latest: Pulling from library/debian

be2ea06d55bb: Pull complete


 Digest:
 sha256:92fd0df2503ccfcb2b122dc0b8e3c27
 f08382d7a787907acb64ceef473f0ad89Statu
 s:    Downloaded    newer    image    for
 debian:latest

 docker.io/library/debian:latest
```

Once the download completes, create a YAML file that's used to define the launch of Nginx container and the Debian image.

```
touch two-container-pod.yaml
```

```
nano two-container-pod.yaml
```

Edit and enter the config shown below:

```
apiVersion: v1

kind: Pod

metadata:

  name: two-containers

spec:

  restartPolicy: Never

  volumes:
```

```yaml
- name: shared-data
  emptyDir: {}
containers:
- name: nginx-container
  image: nginx
  volumeMounts:
  - name: shared-data
    mountPath: /usr/share/nginx/html
- name: debian-container
  image: debian

    volumeMounts:
    - name: shared-data
      mountPath: /pod-data
    command: ["/bin/sh"]
    args: ["-c", "echo Hello from the debian      container      >      /pod-data/index.html"]
```

Next, we can run the `kubectl apply` command to launch the two-containers:

```
kubectl   apply   -f   ~/two-containers-
pod.yaml

pod/two-containers created
```

Once the command executes, use the command below to confirm and view the information about the pod and containers in it.

```
kubectl    get    pod    two-containers    -
output=json

{

    "apiVersion": "v1",

    "kind": "Pod",

    "metadata": {

        "annotations": {

            "kubectl.kubernetes.io/last-
applied-configuration":
"{\"apiVersion\":\"v1\",\"kind\":\"Pod
\",\"metadata\":{\"annotations\":{},\"
name\":\"two-
containers\",\"namespace\":\"default\"
},\"spec\":{\"containers\":[{\"image\"
:\"nginx\",\"name\":\"nginx-
container\",\"volumeMounts\":[{\"mount
```

Path\":\"/usr/share/nginx/html\",\"nam
e\":\"shared-data\"}]},{\"args\":[\"-
c\",\"echo   Hello   from   the   debian
container   \\u003e   /pod-
data/index.html\"],\"command\":[\"/bin
/sh\"],\"image\":\"debian\",\"name\":\
"debian-
container\",\"volumeMounts\":[{\"mount
Path\":\"/pod-
data\",\"name\":\"shared-
data\"}]}],\"restartPolicy\":\"Never\"
,\"volumes\":[{\"emptyDir\":{},\"name\
":\"shared-data\"}]}}\n",

        "kubernetes.io/limit-ranger":
"LimitRanger plugin set: cpu request
for   container\nnginx-container;   cpu
request   for   container   debian-
container"

     },

     "creationTimestamp":   "2020-05-
14T23:39:20Z",

     "name": "two-containers",

     "namespace": "default",

```
    "resourceVersion": "72783",

    "selfLink":
"/api/v1/namespaces/default/pods/two-
containers",

    "uid": "2237d693-963c-11ea-8c4f-
42010af001ca"

    },

  "spec": {

    "containers": [

        {

            "image": "nginx",

            "imagePullPolicy":
"Always",

            "name": "nginx-container",

            "resources": {

                "requests": {

                    "cpu": "100m"

                }

            },
```

```json
            "terminationMessagePath":
"/dev/termination-log",

"terminationMessagePolicy": "File",
            "volumeMounts": [
                {
                    "mountPath":
"/usr/share/nginx/html",
                    "name":      "shared-
data"
                },
                {
                    "mountPath":
"/var/run/secrets/kubernetes.io/servic
eaccount",
                    "name":      "default-
token-rs24n",
                    "readOnly": true
                }
            ]
```

```
        },

        {

            "args": [

                "-c",

                "echo Hello from the
debian container > /pod-
data/index.html"

            ],

            "command": [

                "/bin/sh"

            ],

            "image": "debian",

            "imagePullPolicy":
"Always",

            "name": "debian-
container",

            "resources": {

                "requests": {

                    "cpu": "100m"
```

```
                    }

                },

            "terminationMessagePath":
"/dev/termination-log",


"terminationMessagePolicy": "File",

                "volumeMounts": [

                    {

                        "mountPath":    "/pod-
data",

                        "name":       "shared-
data"

                    },

                    {

                        "mountPath":
"/var/run/secrets/kubernetes.io/servic
eaccount",

                        "name":      "default-
token-rs24n",

                        "readOnly": true
```

```
            }

        ]

      }

  ],

  "dnsPolicy": "ClusterFirst",

  "enableServiceLinks": true,

  "nodeName":              "gke-main-
kubernetes-clus-default-pool-58547964-
p8h1",

  "priority": 0,

  "restartPolicy": "Never",

  "schedulerName":         "default-
scheduler",

  "securityContext": {},

  "serviceAccount": "default",

  "serviceAccountName": "default",

  "terminationGracePeriodSeconds":
30,

  "tolerations": [
```

```json
            {

                "effect": "NoExecute",

                "key":
"node.kubernetes.io/not-ready",

                "operator": "Exists",

                "tolerationSeconds": 300

            },

            {

                "effect": "NoExecute",

                "key":
"node.kubernetes.io/unreachable",

                "operator": "Exists",

                "tolerationSeconds": 300

            }

        ],

        "volumes": [

            {

                "emptyDir": {},
```

```
        "name": "shared-data"

    },

    {

        "name":      "default-token-
rs24n",

        "secret": {

            "defaultMode": 420,

            "secretName": "default-
token-rs24n"

        }

    }

]

},

"status": {

    "conditions": [

        {

            "lastProbeTime": null,

            "lastTransitionTime":
"2020-05-14T23:39:20Z",
```

```
        "type": "Initialized"

    },

    {

        "lastProbeTime": null,

        "lastTransitionTime":
"2020-05-14T23:39:20Z",

        "message":     "containers
with    unready    status:    [debian-
container]",

        "reason":
"ContainersNotReady",

        "status": "False",

        "type": "Ready"

    },

    {

        "lastProbeTime": null,

        "lastTransitionTime":
"2020-05-14T23:39:20Z",
```

```json
            "status": "True",

            "type": "Initialized"

        },

        {

            "lastProbeTime": null,

            "lastTransitionTime":
"2020-05-14T23:39:20Z",

            "message":       "containers
with    unready    status:    [debian-
container]",

            "reason":
"ContainersNotReady",

            "status": "False",

            "type": "Ready"

        },

        {

            "lastProbeTime": null,

            "lastTransitionTime":
"2020-05-14T23:39:20Z",
```

            "message":   "containers
with   unready   status: [debian-
container]",

            "reason":
"ContainersNotReady",

            "status": "False",

            "type": "ContainersReady"

        },

        {

            "lastProbeTime": null,

            "lastTransitionTime":
"2020-05-14T23:39:20Z",

            "status": "True",

            "type": "PodScheduled"

        }

    ],

    "containerStatuses": [

        {

        "containerID":
"docker://28fe2f03cfc557d4e33676705762
27a517f85441fc6b8336427a775ccb647dd5",

        "image": "debian:latest",

        "imageID":   "docker-
pullable://debian@sha256:92fd0df2503cc
fcb2b122dc0b8e3c27f08382d7a787907acb64
ceef473f0ad89",

        "lastState": {},

        "name":   "debian-
container",

        "ready": false,

        "restartCount": 0,

        "state": {

          "terminated": {

            "containerID":
"docker://28fe2f03cfc557d4e33676705762
27a517f85441fc6b8336427a775ccb647dd5",

            "exitCode": 0,

            "finishedAt": "2020-
05-14T23:39:32Z",

```
                "reason":
"Completed",

                "startedAt":    "2020-
05-14T23:39:32Z"

                }

            }

        },

        {

        "containerID":
"docker://6173a4710646b436276a4b5cdfcd
6a86299ff59f185c7207e291c6b5b198689b",

            "image": "nginx:latest",

            "imageID":          "docker-
pullable://nginx@sha256:cccef6d6bdea67
1c394956e24b0d0c44cd82dbe83f543a47fdc7
90fadea48422",

            "lastState": {},

            "name": "nginx-container",

            "ready": true,

            "restartCount": 0,
```

```
        "state": {

            "running": {

                "startedAt":    "2020-
05-14T23:39:26Z"

                }

            }

        }

    ],

    "hostIP": "10.128.0.15",

    "phase": "Running",

    "podIP": "10.32.0.10",

    "qosClass": "Burstable",

    "startTime":              "2020-05-
14T23:39:20Z"

    }

}
```

To verify that the pod is running with the two containers, we use the command:

```
kubectl  exec  -it  two-containers  -c
nginx-container -- /bin/bash
```

This launches a shell that allows us to execute commands. We can test that nginx is running by using the commands:

```
root@xxx:/# apt-get update
```

```
root@xxx:/# apt-get install curl procps -y
```

```
root@xxx:/# ps aux | grep nginx
```

If Nginx is running, you should get an output like the one shown below:

```
root        1 0.0 0.1 10636 5452 ?      Ss  23:39  0:00 nginx: master process nginx -g daemon off;
nginx       6 0.0 0.0 11088 2568 ?      S   23:39  0:00 nginx: worker process
root     2798 0.0 0.0  3084  892 pts/0  S+  23:55  0:00 grep nginx
```

Test message using `curl`.

```
curl -L 127.0.0.1:80
```

```
root@two-containers:/# curl -L 127.0.0.1:80
Hello from the debian container
```

Congratulations, we have confirmed that the Pod we created Links two containers i.e. Nginx and Debian using the same network namespace.

We have executed a lot of commands and a lot of theory. How does all this work in the backend?

Here's an explanation:

Explanation: How Containers Run

Upon executing the commands to create a pod, the Kubernetes scheduling daemon automatically reports the kubelet process.

The kubelet process handles all the operations necessary to launch the two containers `nginx` and `Debian` on one node.

The diagram below shows how the two containers share a common network namespace —or the same interface— thus communicating with each other.

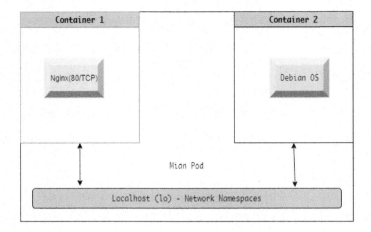

If you are running more than two nodes, you can pass the -o wide flag to the `kubectl get` command to show which node is managing a particular Pod.

You can also create another pod using `nginx` and ubuntu or centos by modifying the yaml file. If successful, you should get two pods, each having two containers running in one cluster.

To delete pods, use the command `kubectl delete pods [pod_name]`. You can also specify `kubectl delete pods -all` to delete all pods within the cluster.

NOTE: Use the latter command with caution.

ReplicaSet

In this sub-section, we are going to cover what ReplicaSets are, how they work, when to use them, and discuss how to use ReplicaSets to manage pods.

Simplified, a ReplicaSet refers to API objects used to keep a set of replica pods running at a stable state at any time.

The ReplicaSet ensures the specified, identical pods are available.

If a pod —or pods— within a ReplicaSet terminate or stop working, the Kubernetes system automatically recreates the pods with the original configurations on a healthy node. Because of this feature, you can always rely on the ReplicaSet to auto-recover and even scale their applications.

Let us start learning how to manage pods with ReplicaSets.

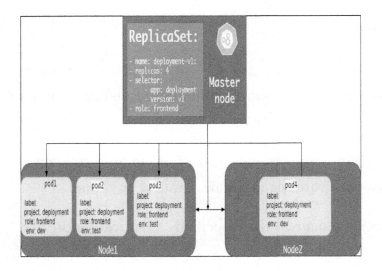

The ReplicaSet is responsible for handling a layer of applications and managing them. In the diagram above, the ReplicaSet is handling four pods. The master node connects to node1 and node2, which in turn contains 3 pods and 1 pod, respectively.

A ReplicaSet has various fields that include a selector field that specifies how to identify pods it acquires. The number of replicas field is important because it indicates how many pods the ReplicaSet should maintain.

The template field specifies the data of new pods that it should create so as to meet the number of replica standards.

The ReplicaSet performs its tasks by deleting and creating the tasks required to reach the desired number of replica pods.

The Pods link to the ReplicaSet using the Pod's `metadata.ownerReferences` (https://kubernetes.io/docs/concepts/workloads/controllers/garbage-collection/#owners-and-dependents) field. This field also specifies the resource the current object is owned by.

Working with ReplicaSets

We create ReplicaSets the same way we create any Kubernetes resource. Using the `kubectl` command on the Kubernetes master ensures that the Kubernetes environment is ready. The Kubernetes node should also access the Docker Hub.

Creating Kubernetes ReplicaSets

By default, running the command `kubectl create` will automatically create a deployment, not a standalone ReplicaSet.

To create a standalone, we can modify the YAML file and enter our configuration as shown below:

```
touch nginx-replica.yaml

nano nginx-replica.yaml
```

Enter the configuration below as is; - modify to your liking.

```
apiVersion: apps/v1

kind: ReplicaSet

metadata:

  name: frontend

  labels:

    app: guestbook

    tier: frontend

spec:

  replicas: 3

  selector:

    matchLabels:
```

```
    tier: frontend

  template:

    metadata:

      labels:

        tier: frontend

    spec:

      containers:

      - name: nginx

        image: nginx:latest
```

Next, we can create the replica using the command:

```
kubectl apply -f nginx-replica.yaml

replicaset.apps/frontend created
```

Once we submit the yaml file to Kubernetes cluster, it creates the defined ReplicaSet and the Pods.

To get the ReplicaSet deployed: use the command:

```
Kubectl get replicaset

NAME            DESIRED    CURRENT    READY
AGE

frontend        3                     3          3
7s
```

The above command shows that the Pods created using the ReplicaSet defined in the YAML file are up and running successfully.

For more detailed information about the ReplicaSet, use the command:

```
kubectl                          describe
replicaset/<ReplicaSetName>
```

Shown below:

```
Kubectl get replicaset/frontend

Name:           frontend

Namespace:      default

Selector:       tier=frontend
```

Kubernetes

```
Labels:         app=guestbook

                tier=frontend

Annotations:
kubectl.kubernetes.io/last-applied-
configuration:


{"apiVersion":"apps/v1","kind":"Replic
aSet","metadata":{"annotations":{},"la
bels":{"app":"guestbook","tier":"front
end"},"name":"frontend",...

Replicas:       3 current / 3 desired

Pods Status:   3 Running / 0 Waiting /
0 Succeeded / 0 Failed

Pod Template:

  Labels:  tier=frontend

  Containers:

   Nginx-server:

    Image:          nginx:latest

    Port:           <none>

    Host Port:      <none>
```

```
   Environment:    <none>

   Mounts:         <none>

   Volumes:        <none>

Events:

   Type       Reason                Age    From
Message

   ----       ------                ----   ----
-------

   Normal     SuccessfulCreate      10h
replicaset-controller    Created  pod:
frontend-vd9rc

   Normal     SuccessfulCreate      10h
replicaset-controller    Created  pod:
frontend-7854v

   Normal     SuccessfulCreate      10h
replicaset-controller    Created  pod:
frontend-9xdfn
```

To check the status of the created pods, use the command:

```
kubectl get pods

NAME                     READY      STATUS
RESTARTS     AGE

frontend-7854v           1/1        Running
0            14m

frontend-9xdfn           1/1        Running
0            14m

frontend-vd9rc           1/1        Running
0            14m
```

Modifying ReplicaSet configuration

We can modify the configuration of Kubernetes resources using the edit, patch, and replace subcommands. These subcommands change the settings of live Kubernetes resources by editing their configuration files.

Let us edit the configuration file of the Kubernetes ReplicaSet we created using the command: `kubectl edit replicaset <replicasetName>`. This command opens the configuration in the default editor, allowing us to modify the YAML configuration. Ensure to check YAML configuration style to avoid errors.

```
# Please edit the object below. Lines beginning with a '#' will be ignored,
# and an empty file will abort the edit. If an error occurs while saving this file will be
# reopened with the relevant failures.
#
apiVersion: extensions/v1beta1
kind: ReplicaSet
metadata:
  annotations:
    kubectl.kubernetes.io/last-applied-configuration: |
      {"apiVersion":"apps/v1","kind":"ReplicaSet","metadata":{"annotations":{},"labels":{"app":"guestbook","tier":"frontend"},"name":"frontend","namespace":"default"},"
    creationTimestamp: "2020-05-15T21:43:30Z"
  generation: 1
  labels:
    app: guestbook
    tier: frontend
  name: frontend
  namespace: default
  resourceVersion: "125093"
  selfLink: /apis/extensions/v1beta1/namespaces/default/replicasets/frontend
  uid: c3070fdb-3bba-4ef7-b546-c7cce032d7c7
spec:
  replicas: 6
  selector:
    matchLabels:
      tier: frontend
  template:
    metadata:
      creationTimestamp: null
      labels:
        tier: frontend
    spec:
      containers:
      - image: nginx:latest
        imagePullPolicy: Always
        name: nginx
        resources: {}
```

Once you modify the required changes, close the editor. The changes will apply automatically.

In the above configuration, we changed the number of replicas from 3 to 6.

View the change by viewing the number of running replicas:

```
kubectl get replicaset
```

NAME	DESIRED	CURRENT	READY	AGE
frontend	6	6	6	37m

You can also try modifying other values within the configuration file.

Destroying ReplicaSets

To remove ReplicaSets, you use the subcommand delete. The command forcefully removes the specified resource from the Kubernetes System.

```
kubectl delete rs frontend

kubectl get pod

replicaset.extensions "frontend" deleted
```

NAME	READY	STATUS	RESTARTS	AGE
frontend-2xzmw	1/1	Terminating	0	7m27s
frontend-7854v	1/1	Terminating	0	41m
frontend-9xdfn	1/1	Terminating	0	41m
frontend-rj695	1/1	Terminating	0	7m27s
frontend-vd9rc	1/1	Terminating	0	41m

```
two-containers              1/2        Running        0
8h

two-containers-four    1/4        Running        0
8h

two-containers-two     1/2        Running        0
8h
```

It's good to note that you cannot scale down a ReplicaSet by deleting a pod within it. The ReplicaSet is a stable management controller. That means if the number of pods specified in the configuration file is not enough, the control manager automatically instructs the ReplicaSet to initialize a new one using the configuration.

The following concept illustrates this best:

First, get all the running pods:

```
kubectl get replicaset, pods
```

NAME	DESIRED	CURRENT	READY
AGE			
replicaset.extensions/frontend	3	3	3
33s			

NAME	READY	STATUS	RESTARTS	AGE
pod/frontend-dsxr4	1/1	Running	0	34s
pod/frontend-st7ct	1/1	Running	0	34s
pod/frontend-wc7ht	1/1	Running	0	34s
pod/two-containers	1/2	Running	0	9h
pod/two-containers-four	1/4	Running	0	8h
pod/two-containers-two	1/2	Running	0	9h

If we try to delete one of the pods, a new pod will automatically initialize.

```
kubectl delete pod frontend-dsxr4

pod "frontend-dsxr4" deleted
```

Now, if we get the replicaset and the pods running, a new one automatically materializes.

```
kubectl get replicaset, pods
```

NAME	DESIRED	CURRENT	READY
AGE			
replicaset.extensions/frontend	3	3	3
5m4s			

NAME	READY	STATUS	RESTARTS	AGE
pod/frontend-176nx	1/1	Running	0	81s
pod/frontend-st7ct	1/1	Running	0	5m5s
pod/frontend-wc7ht	1/1	Running	0	5m5s
pod/two-containers	1/2	Running	0	9h
pod/two-containers-four	1/4	Running	0	8h
pod/two-containers-two	1/2	Running	0	9h

After deleting the pod/frontend-dsxr4, a new pod/frontend-176nx becomes created automatically and attached to the frontend ReplicaSet.

For more detailed information, you can check the log.

Kubernetes

```
λ kubectl describe replicaset frontend

Name:          frontend

Namespace:     default

Selector:      tier=frontend

Labels:        app=guestbook

               tier=frontend

Annotations:   Replicas:  3 current / 3
desired

Pods Status:   3 Running / 0 Waiting /
0 Succeeded / 0 Failed

Pod Template:

  Labels:  tier=frontend
```

```
Containers:

 nginx:

   Image:          nginx:latest

   Port:           <none>

   Host Port:      <none>

   Environment:    <none>

   Mounts:         <none>

 Volumes:          <none>

Events:

  Type      Reason              Age    From
Message

  ----      ------              ----   ----
-------
```

```
  Normal        SuccessfulCreate       10h
replicaset-controller     Created  pod:
frontend-st7ct

  Normal        SuccessfulCreate       10h
replicaset-controller     Created  pod:
frontend-wc7ht

  Normal        SuccessfulCreate       10h
replicaset-controller     Created  pod:
frontend-dsxr4

  Normal        SuccessfulCreate       10h
replicaset-controller     Created  pod:
frontend-176nx
```

ReplicaSets have many similarities with ReplicationControllers. That's because ReplicaSets are successors to ReplicationControllers.

Although they serve the same purpose and function similarly, ReplicationControllers do not support set-based selector requirements. Therefore, it is better to use ReplicaSets to ReplicationControllers.

To learn more about ReplicationControllers, check out the documentation available from the resource below:

https://kubernetes.io/docs/concepts/workloads/controllers/
replicationcontroller/

Deployments

Now that we have discussed ReplicaSets, we can learn about Deployments and Deployment APIs in Kubernetes.

A deployment API ensures that ReplicaSets and Pods have declarative updates.

The deployment controller makes it possible to control the rate at which the present state changes to the desired one; in this case, the desired state is described in a Deployment.

You can use defined deployments to generate new ReplicaSets. Alternatively, you can use them to remove the deployments and adapt their resources to new Deployments

Uses of Deployments

Deployments are useful in the following cases:

- Cleaning up old ReplicaSets not required anymore

- When scaling up deployments to handle more load

- Pausing the deployment to apply fixes and updates to the PodTemplateSpec

- Rolling back to earlier deployment version

- Declaring new states of the pods

Creating a new Deployment

For us to create a deployment, we use the kubectl apply and pass a YAML configuration for Kubernetes to use.

In this case, we are going to create an nginx deployment called nginx-deployment using a YAML configuration file.

```
touch nginx-deployement.yaml

nano nginx-deployment.yaml

apiVersion: apps/v1

kind: Deployment

metadata:

  name: nginx-deployment

  labels:
```

```yaml
    app: nginx
spec:
  replicas: 3
  selector:
    matchLabels:
      app: nginx
  template:
    metadata:
      labels:
        app: nginx
    spec:
      containers:
      - name: nginx
        image: nginx:latest
        ports:
        - containerPort: 80
```
```
kubectl apply -f nginx-deployment.yaml
```

```
deployment.apps/nginx-deployment
created
```

`metadata.name`: This field defines the name of the deployment – nginx-deployment in this case.

`spec.replicas`: This field defines the number of pods created by the deployment.

`spec.selector`: This field defines the method the deployment uses to find the pods it should manage. Controls ReplicaSet/Pods that hold that label.

The template field defines two more sub-fields. The app: nginx labels the pods using the `metadata.labels` field

The pod template specification in the `template.spec` field indicates that the pods run the nginx-container using the `nginx image:latest`

Finally, the:

`spec.template.spec.container[0]` field creates one container and names it nginx, allows the ReplicaSet to manage Pods that contains: the name as nginx, image as nginx:latest and port 80.

Once the command executes, you can check whether the creation of the deployment has used `kubectl get deployements`.

```
kubectl get deployments

NAME                    READY     UP-TO-DATE
AVAILABLE     AGE

nginx-deployment          3/3              3
3             1s
```

You can inspect the deployment using the describe command shown below:

```
kubectl describe deployments nginx-deployment

Name:                          nginx-deployment

Namespace:             default

CreationTimestamp:       Fri, 15 May
2020 16:36:58 -0700

Labels:                  app=nginx
```

Kubernetes

```
Annotations:
deployment.kubernetes.io/revision: 1

Selector:               app=nginx

Replicas:                3 desired | 3
updated | 3 total | 2 available | 1
unavailable

StrategyType:           RollingUpdate

MinReadySeconds:        0

RollingUpdateStrategy:      25%    max
unavailable, 25% max surge

Pod Template:

  Labels:  app=nginx

  Containers:

   nginx:

    Image:          nginx:1.14.2

    Port:           80/TCP

    Host Port:      0/TCP

    Environment:    <none>

    Mounts:         <none>
```

```
  Volumes:           <none>

Conditions:

  Type              Status   Reason

  ----              ------   ------

  Available                      True
MinimumReplicasAvailable

  Progressing                    True
ProgressDeadlineAvailable

OldReplicaSets:  <none>

NewReplicaSet:       nginx-deployment-
7fd6966748 (3/3 replicas created)

Events:

  Type       Reason                 Age
From                  Message

  ----      ------                ----   ---
-                    -------

  Normal     ScalingReplicaSet      10h
deployment-controller      Scaled   up
replica      set      nginx-deployment-
7fd6966748 to 3
```

You can view the deployment rollout status by running the command:

```
kubectl rollout status deployment.v1.apps/nginx-deployment

deployment "nginx-deployment" successfully rolled out
```

Running describe on the ReplicaSet displays fields such as:

NAME: shows the names of the ReplicaSets in the namespace

DESIRED: shows the number of desired replicas in the application, which is the desired state.

CURRENT: shows how many replicas of the application are available. If not achieved, the Replica shows an error.

AGE: shows the amount of time the applications have been up and running.

Accessing applications from various locations may cause a time difference. In this case, there is a 10h difference between the local pc and the cloud cluster.

You can view the labels generated for each pod by running the command:

```
kubectl get pod --show-labels

NAME                                READY   STATUS    RESTARTS
AGE    LABELS

nginx-deployment-68c7f5464c-897w5   1/1           Running     0
13m    app=nginx,pod-template-hash=68c7f5464c

nginx-deployment-68c7f5464c-btcq7   1/1           Running     0
13m    app=nginx,pod-template-hash=68c7f5464c

nginx-deployment-68c7f5464c-nxwcs   1/1           Running     0
13m    app=nginx,pod-template-hash=68c7f5464c
```

The figure below explains the relationship between the deployment, pods, and the ReplicaSet.

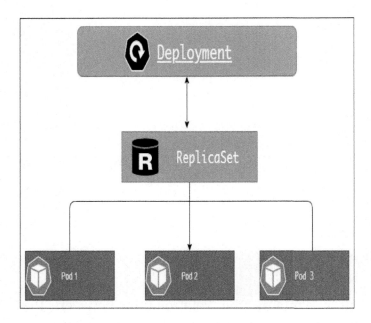

Based on this relationship, an action such as delete on nginx-deployment deployment object, a ripple effect on the ReplicaSet, and the Pods will automatically apply.

```
kubectl delete deployment nginx-deployment

deployment.extensions "nginx-deployment" deleted

kubectl get rs,pods

No resources found in default namespace.
```

That is an example of `create` and `delete`. Deployment objects manage more than one ReplicaSet and thus applies a 1:N relationship.

For example, the Deployment shown below manages 4 ReplicaSets, and each ReplicaSet can manage its own Pod set as indicated in the diagram below:

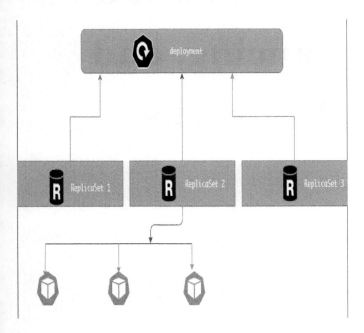

In this section, we covered deployments and how to manage Pods using ReplicaSets. Deployments are very important features in Kubernetes; they allow you to perform rollout and rollback functions.

Section 5

Working with Services, Load Balancing, and Networks

In this section, we are going to cover Kubernetes Services, Networking, and Load Balancing. These essential concepts are very useful in the real world; understanding them will greatly help you work with Kubernetes.

Kubernetes Services

As we defined earlier, a service refers to a way or functionality to expose an application running on a set of pods for external access as a network service running on the cluster.

Kubernetes allows you to use familiar application mechanisms by providing each pod with a unique IP address and a DNS name for a set of pods allowing for load balancing across the nodes.

Types of Kubernetes Services

There are four types of Kubernetes services:

1. **Load Balancer:** A cloud provider's load balancer makes it possible to access a service from outside (externally). An external-based load balancer makes the clusterIP and NodePort created automatically discoverable.

2. **ClusterIP:** This is the default type of service. It ensures that the service is accessible on the cluster internal IP address. This service is only accessible within the cluster.

3. **NodePort:** The NodePort service type exposes the cluster's service on every node's Internet Protocol on a static port. The Node service routes to the ClusterIP service, whose creation is automatic. You can use <NodeIP>:<NodePort> to access the node cluster externally.

4. **ExternalName:** External name maps a service content to the externalName field. It returns a CNAME record value. Support for ExternalName type

is only on kube-dns version 1.7 or higher and coreDNS 0.0.8

You can also use ingress to expose a service within the cluster. Ingress acts as an entry point, not a service type that allows you to combine the routing rules into a single resource. This functionality enables an ingress to expose multiple services under one IP address.

Before going into creating services, let us discuss the kube-proxy daemon.

Kube-proxy

Kube-proxy daemon runs on every node and allocates Virtual IP addresses for all service types except ExternalName service type.

You can set the Kube-proxy various modes:

- **Userspace:** In this mode, the kube-proxy daemon checks the Kubernetes master for services and endpoint objects added. After the discovery of a new service, a port opens up in the local node, and connections directed to the proxy-port are substituted to the pods holding that service and reported to the endpoints.

- **Iptables**: In the iptables mode, the kube-proxy monitors the Master node for added or delete services and endpoint objects but unlike userspace, in iptables mode:

  a. For each service, iptables rules are installed, allowing for the capture of traffic to the service ClusterIP and respective port. The traffic is then captured and redirected to the node.

  b. On every endpoint object created, iptables rules are installed to select a random node at the backend.

- **Ipvs mode:** In the IPVS mode, the kube-proxy daemon monitors the services and endpoint objects and calls the netlink interface to create the appropriate ipvs rules. The ipvs mode also automatically and periodically syncs the ipvs rules with the services and endpoint objects to ensure that the ipvs status is consistent with the expectations. This mode automatically redirects the traffic to a backend pod if the service is accessed.

Discovering Services on Kubernetes

We have briefly seen how to discover services in previous sections.

In this sub-section, we will learn how to use DNS and ENV Var method to access services within Kubernetes.

DNS

Accessing services via DNS is the recommended method of finding services. You should set up a DNS service for the Kubernetes cluster using add-ons. On the cloud, the creation of the DNS service is automatic.

Kubernetes

```
kubectl cluster-info
```

Kubernetes master is running at https://35.227.79.238

GLBCDefaultBackend is running at https://35.227.79.238/api/v1/namespaces/kube-system/services/default-http-backend:http/proxy

Heapster is running at https://35.227.79.238/api/v1/namespaces/kube-system/services/heapster/proxy

KubeDNS is running at

---

https://35.227.79.238/api/v1/namespaces/kube-system/services/kube-dns:dns/proxy

Metrics-server is running at https://35.227.79.238/api/v1/namespaces/kube-system/services/https:metrics-server:/proxy

```
A cluster-aware DNS server constantly monitors for newly created
and deleted services and automatically updates DNS records for
them. |
```

If the DNS server remains enabled throughout the cluster, all pods and nodes should automatically resolve services by basically referencing their names.

The Kubernetes DNS server is the only way that allows access to the ExternalName Service type

Environment Variables ENV Var

Running a pod on a Kubernetes node automatically creates a collection of environment variables for every active service within the pod. Both Docker link variables and simpler {SVCNAME}_SERVICE_PORT, {SVCNAME}_SERVICE_HOST variables are supported by the node. The Service name is upper-cased and the dashed changed to underscores.

Headless Services

Headless services are another type of services used when you do not want a ClusterIP or a load balancing service. Their creation occurs by specifying the −none option in the spec.ClusterIP field of the configuration file.

Headless service comes in two:

- **Headless services with selectors:** Here, the endpoint controllers generates endpoint records, modifying the DNS configurations to yield A value records, which in turn points to pods supporting the service runtime.

- **Headless Services without selectors:** These do not utilize the endpoint controllers. The DNS system takes over the process of configuring CNAME records for ExternalName service type and endpoints that use the same names resources as the services.

Creating a service requires that we expose one of the deployments we created in earlier sections of the book.

We can either use a YAML configuration file for the deployment and apply it, or use the kubectl expose. For the sake of simplicity, we will use the direct command:

```
kubectl expose deployment "nginx-server" -type=ClusterIP -
name="nginx-server"

service "nginx-server" exposed
```

Once the service becomes exposed, we can access the service by running the command `kubectl get services` and get the port number of the service.

Next, we can call the port-forward command to expose the service to external access outside the cluster.

```
kubectl get service nginx-server

NAME                TYPE        CLUSTER-IP      EXTERNAL-IP
PORT(S)     AGE

Nginx-server    ClusterIP   34.20.174.254   <none>        80/TCP
77h

Using the command kubectl port-forward service/nginx-server 80:80

Forwarding from 127.0.0.1:80 -> 80
```

You can then point your browser to the External IP:port to see the nginx welcome page.

Conclusion

Thank you for reading this guide. I hope that you found it extremely educational and easy to implement.

Keep in mind that mastering Kubernetes comes down to practice. The more you practice what you have learned, the better you'll become, and the more comfortable you shall be when learning advanced subjects such as Volumes, Storages, Selectors Scheduling, Security, etc.

I'd like your feedback. If you are happy with this book, please leave a review on Amazon.

Please leave a review for this book on Amazon by visiting the page below:

https://amzn.to/2VMR5qr

Printed in Great Britain
by Amazon

41431734R00111